If Prison Walls Could Speak

RICHARD WURMBRAND

Living Sacrifice Book Company
Bartlesville, OK

If Prison Walls Could Speak

Living Sacrifice Book Company
P.O. Box 2273
Bartlesville, OK 74005-2273 U.S.A.

Design and production by Genesis Group

Cover by David Marty Design

Printed in the United States of America

Reprinted December 2005

ISBN 0-88264-305-3

Unless otherwise indicated, Scripture references are from the *New King James* version, © 1979, 1980, 1982 by Thomas Nelson Inc., Publishers, Nashville, Tennessee.

Scripture references marked KJV are from the *King James* version.

Contents

Preface

THROW A CHRISTIAN into the river, and he will come up with a fish in his mouth. I have not known a Christian who remained faithful through adversities and inner struggles who did not come out of them enriched.

When I was released from prison, I brought with me a treasure that God had given me there: three hundred and fifty-six poems, which were condensations of sermons that I composed while alone in a cell.

I published some of them in my book *With God in Solitary Confinement*. They were well received, and many people have written to tell me that they have been helped by reading them. This encouraged me to publish another volume of these sermons written when I had no pen or paper, and delivered to an invisible audience. I was imprisoned underground. I saw no one except the guards and the examining officers. I entrusted my sermons to the Holy Spirit. He could take my words to my brothers and sisters in the faith.

God has done far more than I asked of Him. He always does. He released me from prison, brought me to the free world, and gave me opportunities to publish in many languages my experiences in prison. Let me be more precise. I do not publish the experiences, but the words in which these experiences are expressed.

There is a big difference.

When missionary John G. Paton tried to translate the New Testament for the people of New Hebrides, he found that they had no word in their language for "faith." Instead, he used a word that means literally "to repose quietly, without worrying, on the grass." So those who read John 3:16 in the New Hebrides understand that a man who rests serenely, without fretting, on the fact that God gave His Son for him, will have eternal life. In Central Africa, other translators have used a word meaning "to hear and to do," which is the exact opposite. The Hebrew word for faith, *emunah*, or the Hausa, *amince*, both mean "to say amen."

When I read the word for "holy" in Hebrew, *kadosh*, I know it comes from the same stem as the word for "prostitute," which helps me to understand that a saint is a man who offers himself spiritually to everybody and embraces everybody in love, without distinction of age, physical or moral qualities, race or creed. When I read the Greek word for "holy," *aghios*, which means literally "not of the earth (*ghea*)," I understand that a saint is a man detached from earthly things. In different languages, words convey different sentiments.

On the one hand there is your experience, and on the other hand a very poor attempt to put it into words developed by men whose experiences have been totally unlike yours.

To give a true account of my own experiences as a man tortured, mocked, and drugged in a solitary cell, I would have to invent words of my own; but then I could not communicate.

We did not live in the sphere of words there. The apostle John says that on Patmos he saw. We can put into words what we saw only in the measure in which we could describe to a blind man Michelangelo's *Pieta*, or Leonardo's Mona Lisa.

D. L. Moody said that the Christian on his knees sees more than a philosopher standing on tiptoe. If you want to know what hundreds of thousands of Christians have experienced, and are still experiencing, in Communist prisons, don't stop at reading these sermons. Get down on your knees and ask God for the privilege of sharing the cross of the sufferers, of remembering them as though you were bound in chains with them.

But don't share only the outward physical suffering, the hunger, the tortures. Share what is far worse: the inner tempest, the doubts, the moments of despair.

These sermons are not what we usually understand by a sermon—the proclamation of God's truth—but are an attempt to make others feel the storms of doubt, and sometimes even of rebellion against God, which assail a prisoner under such conditions. These doubts assailed John the Baptist when he knew that Jesus was living not far from his prison yet never came to visit him. They forced Christ Himself to ask God why He had forsaken Him. Under normal circumstances, it would be blasphemy to suggest that the heavenly Father could give up a righteous man. But Jesus was not preaching on the cross as priests do from their pulpits. He was experiencing suffering—the greatest mystery in the good and almighty God's creation—and was expressing what he felt at that moment when He cried, "My God, My God, why have You forsaken Me?" (Matthew 27:46).

There are not enough shovels on earth to bury the truth. And there are no pains enough to prevent truth and faith and love from triumphing at last, even when you pass through the worst temptations. I have doubted, I have had moments of despair, but these were all overcome. The sermons finish on a note of victory. I left prison still a Christian.

I was set free. Others have remained in captivity. Watchman Nee and Wang-Min-Dao were in prison in China for nineteen years, Hrapov in Russia for thirty years. Many have gone into prison since I left it. When you read these sermons, you are reading what is going on in their hearts today. You will thus be able to weep, but also to rejoice with them, and to arrive at some sort of understanding of the life of those who suffer.

I publish these sermons not in order that people should learn Christianity from them. For this they have their pastors. My purpose is to show what Communist imprisonment and torture can do to a Christian's mind and faith.

The Gospel writers found it necessary to publish the doubts that assailed John the Baptist when he was in prison and the distress of Jesus' mind in Gethsemane and on the cross. Their purpose was not to teach you to question whether Jesus is the Messiah, or to consider yourself forsaken by God when you suffer innocently. But it is important for a disciple to know that such doubts can come. It helps him not to be afraid of them when they do come.

I am very well aware that some of the ideas expressed in this book will run counter to the understanding of Scripture which many Christians have. But my life at the time these sermons were composed also ran counter to the life style of Christians in the free world. I had no Bible, no theology books, no Christian fellowship to check whether my thoughts were right. Don't compare my thoughts in a solitary cell with your thoughts when you sit comfortably in a study. Try rather to understand what the millions of Christians in Communist prisons have thought and think when beaten by terrible tempests.

I composed these sermons on the verge of insanity. In the Soviet Union, Christians were placed in asylums, and after a time some of them really went mad. Were their ideas on the last days before they went mad not also a treasure of the church, a treasure that must be kept with respect as a holy thing, though they contradict beliefs of those who never were bound in straitjackets and gagged?

Even theologically sophisticated readers, if they will weep with those who weep instead of judging them as sobbing in an unorthodox manner, should listen to the cries of sufferers. The good Samaritan did not question the orthodoxy of the man who had been beaten by robbers. He helped. It is an essential part of orthodox Christian belief to be silent and to help when men in terrible pain say wrong things.

I will not take the place of your pastor who will be responsible before God for his flock. It is for him to teach you the fundamentals of faith. I wish only to remind you of your brothers and sisters under extreme pressure in Communist jails. Not only their bodies are wounded. Their minds also suffer deformations.

Now when I write down these sermons, kept in my memory during the years, I realize that sometimes they contradict each other. I leave them as they were composed. What man does not have inner contradictions? And if we have them, why pretend to be consistent? It is we who make the Bible consistent. Its authors were too big to waste time on this. They loved God with all their heart, with its good and with its evil side, and allowed both to speak to the glory of God. God accepted it and has caused the bloody psalms of vengeance in the Old Testament and clamor for retaliation in the Book of Revelation to be included in the same book with the poem on love in 1 Corinthians 13.

In these sermons thoughts are expressed that would not occur to a Christian of the free world. But would his thoughts not change if his country fell under a dictatorial rule? Dietrich Bonhoeffer was an evangelical pastor. When his country was under the boot of Hitler he became an agent of the "Abwehr," the Nazi intelligence service. He got orders from this organization to spy on the ecumenical movement. For this purpose he was allowed to contact church leaders of countries that fought against Germany. Using these contacts he served Christ, telling the foreign church leaders of the atrocities of Nazism and what might be done to overthrow it. Then he came back and reported something other than what he had spoken. His only aim in this double play was to help the cause of God and of freedom. In the end he went to prison for his faith and died a martyr's death. Anyone who has not worked in an underground church has to accept that things like this happen, and he is not to judge. When his own church is underground, he will have to do the same.

The thoughts contained in these sermons do not occur to a Christian in the free world, because he has never been alone for years in a Communist jail. Solitary confinement, accompanied by torture, drugging with narcotics, and brainwashing, gives you unique experiences.

We read in 1 Samuel 1:1 that the prophet was from the tribe Ephraim. Then he had a rare experience. God spoke to him when he was only a boy. God who is sovereign raised him to a priestly office, normally reserved for the tribe of Levi. This changed not only his status. In 1 Chronicles 6:33–35 the same five ancestors of Samuel are named, but no more as Ephraimites. When Samuel was changed to the tribe of Levi by a direct call from God, the tribe of his ancestors until the fifth generation has changed too. Now they are numbered among the Levites, just like their descendant.

This is an exceptional happening: a boy's talk with God produced great changes not only for him, but also for those related to him. I'm far from being a Samuel. But I also had a tremendous experience with God in unusual circumstances. It has changed my manner of thinking, my feelings, my relationship with other men. My experience has perhaps also changed the status of some related to me. It has certainly brought with it ferocious attacks of the devil, fierce attempts on his part to suggest wrong thoughts disguised as revelations from God. I have now put on paper everything—what came from God, from the devil, and from me —so that you might understand the terrible battle going on in the minds of those who suffer for Christ today. For many of them the worst pain is not the physical torture, but the intellectual conflict. Dostoevski, who had also been in prison, wrote, "It is not as a child that I believe and confess Jesus Christ. My 'hosanna' is born of a furnace of doubt."

For Samuel the change was a permanent one. He remained a Levite to the end of his life.

Since my release from prison, I have come back to normal conditions of life and to normal thoughts. Today I have the same quiet creed that all evangelical Christians have. Looking back to the thoughts that passed through my mind in solitary confinement, I wonder myself about many of the ideas I nurtured there. I am on the safe side now. But the communion of saints is possible only if we bear with our imprisoned brethren their tempests of doubt and the assaults of the devil. In *Tortured for Christ, In the Face of Surrender*, and other publications, I gave a description of the physical sufferings of the bride of Christ in Communist countries. The other side also had to be told—the story of the mental stress. You need to know the state of their minds when their reason rocks under the pressure of Communist imprisonment.

Read this book with charity toward those who suffer more than words can describe, instead of comparing every assertion with Bible verses. We had no Bibles and had forgotten theology.

CHAPTER 1

The Making of a Messenger

D<small>EAR BROTHERS AND SISTERS</small>,

To what shall I compare my solitary cell?

It is like a wood full of the fragrance of flowers. No tree in the forest gives off a sweeter perfume than the one out of which crosses are made.

To what else shall I compare my cell?

It is like a rich storehouse. The same Greek word translated "closet" in Matthew 6:6 is translated "storehouse" in Luke 12:24. God, the angels, the demons, the saints, my forefathers, my friends and my enemies, all future generations, the whole universe and its Creator are here. There is no joy that I cannot experience by the simple method of rejoicing with those who rejoice. In the spirit, I can accompany others on wonderful journeys, I can share their emotions as they worship in church or enjoy a good meal. I can rejoice with mothers bending over the cribs of their babes. I can play merrily with young children. I can weep with those who weep. Here in my cell I have theology, philosophy, politics, lighthearted jokes and serious projects, virtues and vices.

I could liken my cell to a cinema. "*Vechol haam roim et hako-lot*—and all the people saw the voices" (Exodus 20:18 in the original). In exceptional circumstances, like the terrifying moment when God appeared on Mount Sinai, it is possible to see voices. I used to wonder about that verse when I was free. It was usual for the Jews to listen only. Unhappily, it has remained the usual thing for most Christians also. But it ought not to be so. Christians are meant to be men and women who "behold," if only as in a mirror. They are meant to see the glory of the Lord (2 Corinthians 3:18). Here in my cell I see phantasmagoric moving pictures. Some depict scenes of horror but some are of indescribable beauty, such as I have never known before. And it is not only pictures I can see. What normally would be voices, expressing clear propositions of philosophical, theological, or social content, become images. How much there is to be seen in a solitary cell! It really is true that you are never less alone than when you are alone.

But I would also liken my cell to the studio of a sculptor. Michelangelo looked at a block of marble, and saw an angel. All he had to do was to hew away the superfluous stone. I believe that these cells are places in which the great Sculptor shapes His future messengers.

Supposing that He makes a messenger out of me, what shall I look like? The thought becomes an image. I see myself as I shall be then.

Now I see the person described in Kipling's poem "The Prophet of the Utterly Absurd":

Who, when the thing that couldn't be occurred
Just takes time to change a leg and goes again.

You don't think during tortures. But now, when I think back on them, I find in them a symbolism.

They fix a rope around your manacles. Then you are lifted up in the air so that you cannot reach the ground except on tiptoes. The steel of the manacles cuts into your wrists. You have cramps in your feet for a long time afterward, but you have stretched higher than anybody else. An utterly absurd position, like the prophet's calling.

Supposing, God, that I do become a messenger, will it be a source of joy or pain for me? I will have to receive messages from You. Daniel trembled when he received a revelation from the mysterious being Gabriel, who is simultaneously man (Daniel 9:21) and angel (Luke 1:19). The beloved disciple John fainted when he saw the Lord (Revelation 1:17). I am driven nearly insane at the mere thought of receiving messages for the people directly from You.

Usually, preachers get their messages from books they read, which copied the thoughts of other writers, inspired in their turn by an earlier sermon of Charles Spurgeon, who took his inspiration avowedly from Calvin, who was greatly inspired by John Chrysostom, who learned from men of a former generation how to interpret a message that an apostle received from God. This is a golden chain of tradition through which the truth has been conveyed to us. The church possesses a treasury accumulated over centuries, from which preachers do well to draw. But a messenger from God is a rare phenomenon.

These cells are places in which the great Sculptor shapes His future messengers.

Arius's teaching is so clear, so easily acceptable to the human mind—yet blasphemous. Arius held that Jesus was not God but only the highest of the created beings. And you cannot call St. Athanasius other than utterly absurd. The Athanasian creed makes human reason shudder: "Whosoever will be saved, before all things it is necessary that he hold the Catholic Faith; which Faith except every one do keep whole and undefiled, without doubt he shall perish everlastingly…"

What will the absurdity of my message be? When I see myself as God's messenger, I see two possible Wurmbrands. One plays a role similar to Jeremiah and Gedaliah (2 Kings 25:22), telling Christians what they will never accept, unless perhaps outwardly: that they must submit to the Communist oppressors, as the Jews had to submit to Babylon, and seek the peace of those who subdued them by violence (Jeremiah 29:7). On a practical level, the Jews had no other choice. If they had resisted, Babylon would have utterly destroyed them as a nation. So, the

Communists have the prospect of remaining in power for generations. Should not Christians submit and accept the terrible fact? Much suffering could be avoided if they did. The Communists have proposed that I should play a role similar to that of Jeremiah. The Babylonians would protect me. How ashamed Jeremiah must have been to receive their favor. My brethren would call me a traitor. Yet, notwithstanding, I would be sure that I was a messenger of God. Jeremiah did not doubt his calling, though it was nothing less than what any martial court would condemn as high treason, propaganda made in time of war to submit to the enemy.

Then I see another Wurmbrand who is organizing a Christian fight against communism, in Romania or perhaps abroad—this also could be, because to a messenger the utterly absurd can happen.

These two types are contradictory. I see two Wurmbrands before me. I see them delivering contradictory messages. If each were embodied in different persons, they would have to quarrel publicly. Neither could fulfill his task without the other denouncing him as an evildoer. But there is a high spiritual level on which the two are one.

According to the Jewish Talmud, an animal is unclean for food if it has some stones in the kidneys. "How big must the stone be to make the animal unclean?" asked a rabbi. To which another replied, "The stones must be the size of an olive kernel in one kidney, and another olive kernel in the other." The first rabbi guessed, "You are hiding something from me. It is not about stones in the kidneys that you wish to speak, but about some deep mystery." "You have conjectured rightly," the other answered. "I meant that if there comes a persecution against religion, the rabbis must divide into two camps. Some must accept death and not change even the manner in which we Jews tie our shoelaces. The other group must make friends with the tyrant, compromise with him, in order to win at least some concessions. And the martyrdom of those who pretend to be on good terms with the murderers of Jews is not less than the martyrdom of those who sacrifice themselves on matters of principle. This is the meaning of the size of the stones in an animal's kidneys."

God looks only on the heart. And both Wurmbrands may be right. To say that there is only one truth is like denying the existence of both positive and negative electricity. It shows a lack of understanding of the notion "one," which can only be defined as a synthesis of contradictory forces. That is what *one* atom, or *one* man, is. That is the sense of the word "one" even when applied to God. A Son who prays with bitter tears that He might be spared the cup of suffering, and a Father who says "No" to his agonizing Son, are one God. That is why the Bible calls God by the Hebrew word *ehad*, which means compound oneness, and never by the word *iahid*, which is absolute oneness, uniqueness. Absolute one does not exist.

The Sculptor knows what He will hew from the block of stone that He keeps in this cell. I can see the manifest beauty of the one masterpiece and the veiled beauty of the other. The latter resembles a piece of surreal art—only the initiated can understand it.

But a third image emerges, one that I like more than any other. This is the image of a Wurmbrand who practices no wise policy, who is no warrior—but one who smiles. For centuries Leonardo da Vinci's Mona Lisa has done nothing but smile and make the onlookers just a little bit happier. Isac Feinstein, the man who played a big role in my conversion and who was later killed in a pogrom, had received this message from God. Years after his death, a man to whom I spoke about him said, "Nobody could ever forget his smile." Did he smile like that to the last? The greatest preacher of our country was Brother Paulini, president of the Seventh Day Adventist convention. His message was a smile on a shining face. Such messengers fulfill the words of St. John of the Cross: where there is no love, put love, and love will grow.

It may be that God, like every great sculptor, has several projects, and that the images I see are only provisional drafts of His possible intentions. Or perhaps I shall die in prison, and go to

God as a messenger of mankind, to tell Him that it is much too unhappy to be judged guilty.

We used to read to our little son, Mihai, every day a passage of Scripture and a page from the *Lives of the Saints*. I remember the Christians who were brought before the Roman proconsul Saturninus. Speratus told him, "I do not acknowledge the rulers of this age, but rather I serve the God who has never been seen by men and who cannot be looked on with mortal eyes." Vestia said simply, "I am a Christian." The proconsul wanted to give them time to rethink their attitude. Speratus said, "In a cause so righteous there is no need to rethink." Both were beheaded. Now they serve God day and night in His temple (Revelation 7:15). In what does this service consist, if not in telling God how invincible was the ignorance of their persecutor and how great is the misery of humanity? They do not have to tell God much about God. He knows this better Himself. I would like to be a messenger of mankind to God, as much as to be a messenger of God to mankind.

I will allow God to choose which it is to be.

My brothers and sisters, you also must believe that your lives are clay in the hands of a wonderful Sculptor. He never makes mistakes. If at times He is hard on you, it is because He sometimes has what we could call negative successes. He loses a pawn in order to win the chess game. He loses a battle in order to win a war. He causes his Son to endure suffering in order to save a world. Just trust. Don't live on another's messages, but discover the message for which He is molding you. Amen.

CHAPTER 2

A Joyful Noise Unto the Lord

MYSTERIOUS RULER,

Today it seems quite pointless for me to speak to You.

Humiliation destroys a soul far more easily than torture. This morning the examining officer asked me to open my mouth. They often do this to check that you don't have any poison hidden in it. But when I opened my mouth this time, he spat in it. I swallowed the phlegm.

Then he ordered me to kneel. His warm urine ran down my face. How stupid one can be. The verse which came into my mind at that moment was the one about "the precious oil upon the head, running down on the beard" (Psalm 133:2).

And now I am back in my cell. Should I pray? "Is any among you suffering? Let him pray" (James 5:13). But how can I pray to One who has foreordained all things, who has all power in heaven and in earth, and in whose world someone urinates on my head?

I wonder why I swallowed the phlegm instead of spitting it out. I certainly was not thinking about what I was doing. But we are surrounded by the saints (Hebrews 12:1). I thought of St. Catherine when the officer spat in my mouth. She was a princess who cared for the sick. One of them was full of lice, and she was so overcome by disgust that she almost left him uncared for. So she swallowed a louse taken from his body. This helped. I have always admired her for this. Now perhaps she has taught me to do, just for a moment, something similar.

But his urine on my head was too much. God, I have simply nothing to tell You about it, neither as a reproach, nor by way of thanks. Nor do I wish to embarrass You by asking You the indiscreet question, "Why?" You would perhaps not know the answer.

So I circle around my cell, making a noise that I call joyful. Tra-la-la-la-tum-tum-te-tum-tra-la. Or am I in fact weeping? The Hebrew word *nud* means both "to bemoan" and "to skip for joy." You have asked us to "shout joyfully to the Lord" (Psalm 98:4). Well, here you have it, "Pom-pom-tara-pom-tara." When I am beyond understanding anything, I can enjoy the miracle of hearing my own voice.

I stop making a noise in order to think. Why do You need joyful noises? I prefer the quiet. Perhaps You are stricken by some deep sorrow that we have to cure, as young David had to cheer Saul's melancholy by playing the harp.

Perhaps You are like the ancient Persian kings whose palaces no mourner was allowed to approach. A king needs quiet, and a cool mind, in order to rule a country.

But men are constantly crying out to You in their need. The joyful noises of believers must drown these cries, in order to create in the Godhead the right mood for its own work. It is probably for this reason that the angels sing unceasingly the same praise, "Holy, holy, holy, is the Lord of hosts" (Isaiah 6:3). Some churches repeat over and over again the words, "Glory be to the Father and to the Son and to the Holy Ghost; as it was in the beginning, is now and ever shall be." No one really wants the glory of God to be through all eternity what it is now. It would be a poor thing. But because these songs are being repeated uninterruptedly, You cease to pay attention to them. They become just a joyful noise, a background against which You can continue to think Your own thoughts.

Our job is to create a barrier of noise around You, so that man's cries of despair may not distract You from Your work which alone can destroy the root of all despair.

You must be deeply sad, because You find Yourself in one of four situations:

(1) As Origen taught, You are working with uncreated matter, existing since eternity, in which there is intrinsic evil which you must overcome;

(2) You have Yourself foreordained all the sufferings of the world, including this urine on my head, for an ultimate good purpose. This is a Protestant concept. But I don't know if You agree with the Protestant creed. When the Augsburg and Westminster confessions were drafted, You were not consulted. Anyhow, it must be terrible for You to look at sufferings which You, who are fundamentally good, have foreordained;

(3) Man has free will, and his sufferings are the result of his rebellion against You. Then Your sorrow must be that of a father whose own children are his enemies;

(4) Zoroaster was right, and You have a great adversary who cannot yet be subdued.

You choose. Don't ask me to solve theological problems with this head of mine, which they have abused. I will just make a joyful noise. Tum-tum-te-tum. No words, no tune, no rhythm. Don't even try to find some sense in it. You just mind Your business, which is to create a new kingdom.

The places where I have felt the deepest quiet have been in the Jewish Chassidic synagogues and in Christian Pentecostal meetings, where everyone is shouting at once, in a mixture of voices at different pitches, all saying something different. The unintelligible noise gave me a feeling of inner serenity.

Jesus, on the cross, after having uttered seven statements, did the most beautiful thing of all: "He had cried out again with a loud voice" (Matthew 27:50). What did He cry? It was not a "what." It was just a joyful noise. "Tra-la-la-la. Tra-la—You, Father, just quietly get on with Your own business. I have done My work. I have endured all the mockeries and the pain. I have just one thing more to do: to make a joyful noise. So I will cry aloud." It is only now that I understand this verse. That cry is worth more than all the theories of Origen, Luther, Spurgeon, or anyone else.

If I had to die today, I would like my last breath to be not a prayer or a hymn, but just a joyful noise. The tra-la-la can be joyful because I may meet in heaven the man who humiliated me. He has as many chances of salvation as I have.

I always marveled at the ritual of the Day of Atonement as described in Leviticus 16. The high priest had to cast lots upon two goats: one lot for the Lord and one for the scapegoat (verse 8). The scapegoat was destined for release in the wilderness. If the law had stipulated one hundred lots for the Lord and one for the scapegoat, nobody could have objected. But God is all for fair play. Only one lot for Him, the same as for the scapegoat, not a whit more. His Son was born in a stable, like many poor children. His Son feasted at the banquets of rich tax collectors, as many other men did. His Son died on a cross; so did the robbers. His Son rose from the dead, as millions will also rise. He will keep no privilege for Himself. He is in glory, and "when He is revealed, we shall be like Him" (1 John 3:2)—we, His former enemies. We shall sit with Him on His throne —we, former murderers, liars, adulterers, slanderers, unbelievers. One lot for God; one lot for the scapegoat. There is equality of chances with the Lord.

> We shall sit with Him on His throne—we, former murderers, liars, adulterers, slanderers.

So this officer's chances of going to heaven are equal with mine. I cannot imagine how any conversation between us will be possible there. It will be too difficult for him to apologize; he will not be able to explain or justify his action. I shall not be able to speak any kind words. We shall simply take each other's hands and cry out ecstatically some loud, senseless noise.

Tra-la-te-tum. How wonderful to circle around my cell and make a joyful noise! A pity it cannot be too loud now. The guards would object. Perhaps you will take this noise as a prayer.

Protestants reproach Catholics for praying before statues of the saints. But for me, even such a prayer is more acceptable than one in which a man keeps before his eyes only his own self with its remorse, its troubles, its desires, its ambitions, its needs, and its stupid memories about somebody having reviled him. Is it not much better just to make a joyful noise?

What this officer did to me was base. But God chooses the base things (1 Corinthians 1:28). I will think of him as my future companion in the heavenly choir which will make a joyful noise unto the Lord. Tra-la-la-la. I am calmer now. This also has passed.

I started my first sermon as a young pastor with a story: King David once summoned a jeweler and gave him an order, "Make me a ring which will transform my mood from sorrow to joy or from joy to sorrow whenever I look on it. If you make it within a week, you will be royally rewarded. If not, you will be beheaded." The jeweler left the palace a broken man. He knew that his life was lost. But in the palace courtyard little Solomon was playing. He noticed the sorrow on the man's face and asked him the reason. When the jeweler told him of the king's command, Solomon laughed and said, "You must make a plain ring of tin, and engrave on it the words *Gam ze iavo*—'This also will pass.' That is all. If he looks at it when he is merry, my father will at once become serious, and when he is worried, a look at the ring will wipe the frown from his face."

Gam ze iavo. So many terrible events have passed in my life. Now this has passed, too. With Jesus the incarnation passed, the crucifixion passed. Everything passes. It is as though nothing has happened to me today. My beloved God, let us walk again in companionship with one another. Amen.

CHAPTER 3

My Image

DEAR BROTHERS AND SISTERS,

The examining officer was in a good mood today. You could sense it from the very beginning. There would be no beating. He just wanted to amuse himself with some pleasant conversation.

He asked me, "Do you believe that God created man in His own image?" I answered, "I certainly do." "Do you believe that you are in the image of God?" "Of course."

Then he took a mirror out of his pocket and handed it to me. "Look into the glass. See how ugly you are. You have dark circles under your eyes. You are all skin and bones. Your whole appearance is haggard, like a madman. If you are in the image of God, God must be as ugly as you are. Why should you worship Him?"

I had already seen myself in a mirror once since I had been in jail, and I knew that I was terribly ugly, I who had been considered a handsome man. I had been horrified to see myself in such shape. Now, my ugliness was being made into a theological problem.

Happily, Christians do not have to think beforehand what to answer. The words are given to them.

I said, "Yes, my God has an ugly face like me. In Hebrew there is no such word as 'face.' You can only say 'faces'—*panim*. The word has no singular. There is a deep meaning in this, because no man has only one face. He shows one countenance when he speaks to a superior, another when he bullies an inferior, one when he is grieved, another when he hears good news. Our God also has many faces. One is a face of complete serenity, the serenity of a Being who has foreordained everything and can see from the beginning the happy end of the tortuous road. He has a face radiant with joy, sharing the pleasure of all who rejoice, even that of a little girl who has been given a new doll. But He has also another image, one of even worse suffering and ugliness than mine. We saw this face on Golgotha. His hair was disordered, His brow was disfigured by wounds. Spittle and blood mingled on His face. He had dark circles under His eyes. 'He had no form or comeliness' (Isaiah 53:2). This, too, is one of the faces of the Godhead. Christ is not ashamed to call me His brother."

I hope the Communist officer understood at least something of what I told him.

Now, back in my cell, my thoughts, which are not diverted by new events as they would be if I were free, continue to dwell on the question asked of me. Everyone who suffers bears the image of the God who became "a Man of sorrows and acquainted with grief" (Isaiah 53:3). But what about my soul? God, too, has a soul (Isaiah 42:1; Zechariah 11:8). Is His soul also like mine, a bird that continually flies from place to place, from ugly thoughts to the most lofty and back, tossed to and fro by passions, a mixture of holiness and worldliness? Does my soul, polluted by sin, bear the image of His, as my face, vilified by sufferings, is surely an image of the Godhead; yes, of the Godhead in its highest form—the self-sacrificing Godhead?

Does God also have an ugly soul, like mine?

But how do I know that my soul is ugly? By self-analysis. "Examine yourselves," say the Scriptures (2 Corinthians 13:5). "Know yourself" was the teaching of Socrates. But can we do this?

When I think about myself, as about everything else, I do so in words. The Romanian language has possibly 200,000 words.

So we could not even give a name to all the 30 billions of stars that exist in our galaxy alone, nor to the octillions of atoms that constitute my body. With what poor instrument I think about myself!

How much of my soul is really me, and how much is a legacy from my ancestors?

If Judas Iscariot had examined himself with absolute sincerity, he would have discovered that he was a genuine disciple of Jesus who had sold everything in order to join the group of apostles; that under his preaching men were converted; that, like the other apostles, he had developed a beneficent activity, healing sick people, driving out demons. He had just one besetting sin remaining. But so had his colleagues: a quarrelsome spirit, or pride, or cowardice. Judas's besetting sin was dishonesty in petty things. But there is no man who has not some sin, and with Jesus there is forgiveness. How could Judas have known that the devil had put it into his heart to betray Jesus? What do I know about the imponderable influences of angels and devils in my heart? Their influences have a long incubation period, as with some diseases, and you discover them only years later when they appear in some unexpected outward act.

All psychoanalysts would agree that there is no possibility of a thorough and valid self-examination. The examiner is I. The examined is I. The subjects on which I shall be examined are decided by the teacher, I, with the knowledge of the pupil, I. The examiner is biased. The apparatus with which I examine the I is I. There is not the slightest possibility of achieving an objective result.

A Pharisee examined himself and found that he was a good man. He was mistaken. Close by him, a tax collector examined himself and discovered that he was lost. He, too, was mistaken. He was unable to discover the reality that he was justified. Wisely, Jesus' parable does not tell us that the man ceased to be a tax collector after having beaten his breast about his sin. Neither have I reason to believe that Zacchaeus fulfilled his promise to restore fourfold everything he had stolen. Self-examination can bring a man to beautiful decisions, but not to their fulfillment. The Bible does not tell us that he really gave back the money. We always examine only the superficial strata of our ego. We don't penetrate to its ultimate depths.

The law of Moses was given, not that we should fulfill it, but to make us discover our incapacity to do so. And the Bible says, "Examine yourselves," to make us aware that self-examination is impossible.

The thinker, the subject of his thought, and the act of thinking are one, as God is one.

Why do I believe God to be one, and not two as in Zoroastrianism, or many as in Hinduism? The number one has certain peculiarities. It is the only number that remains the same when you multiply it by itself. God can multiply Himself; He can beget a Son; the Holy Spirit may proceed from Him; then many children can be born from Him and added to the mystical body of Christ. They become partakers of the divine nature. But the One remains one.

> The law of Moses was given, not that we should fulfill it, but to make us discover our incapacity to do so.

One is the only number the root of which is itself. Extract the root of the Godhead, and a Carpenter will tell you, "He who has seen Me has seen the Father" (John 14:9). It makes no difference whether we look at the Creator of the galaxies and of all mankind, or at a Carpenter confined to one room, who is soon to be crucified. The root is equal to the whole number. I may be the millionth root of the One. Yet I am still One, not a particle less.

The definition of the word "number" is a quantity related to one. The number one is the foundation of everything. The faith is one. God is one, Christ is one. I am this one. I died, and it is Christ who lives in me (Galatians 2:20). There is nobody to analyze himself. There is no analyzer and no analyzed. There is only the One God in whom we all live, move, and have our being

(Acts 17:28). We belong to an inner world, of the one Soul, full of beauty. What appears in the distorting mirror of my mind as ugliness is the splendor of His all-understanding and all-pardoning love. My cursed mind considers me ugly. In the eyes of the only One who judges rightly, I am pleasing.

A great miracle occurs. The highest possible beauty, the Godhead, is beautified even more when mirrored in the soul of a bride of Christ, who like Mary of Bethany sits quietly at the feet of Jesus, instead of torturing herself with self-examination, which can result only in pride or despair.

We have to look not at ourselves, but at the bronze serpent. It is this faith which heals (Numbers 21:9). There is no healing in evaluating the number and gravity of the wounds inflicted by the snakes. Look away from the pus and blood, and concentrate upon the One Savior who has taken up residence in you to make you one. One with Him and one with yourself. There is no greater beauty than that of oneness. I have this beauty. Yes, my soul bears His image.

"All things work together for good" (Romans 8:28). St. Augustine adds, "even my sins." The former sins of the woman at the well were the raw material out of which her future faithfulness was produced. The former crimes of Saul of Tarsus were the ingredients for making the most zealous apostle. Some men have to choose their way. Abraham was privileged. About him it is written that God was with him in all that he did (Genesis 21:22).

Be happy, my soul. You bear the beautiful image of God, as God bore your ugly countenance during His crucifixion. Or rather, just because of this.

Don't examine yourselves, my brothers, by criteria chosen by yourself, by a book declared by yourself to be holy (your fellow men do the same thing with the Talmud, the Koran, or the Vedas), according to an interpretation of it chosen by yourself, according to a standard of morality that changes when you cross a frontier or when the century changes. Believe that God blesses you in what you do. The church needed the intransigence of Paul, the courage of the first martyrs, the compromise with the State made in the time of Constantine, the quarrelsome spirit of Luther, the calm of Melanchthon, and the neutrality of Erasmus. The church needs men who choose the way of martyrdom under communism, and also the official church leaders who in good faith serve the same Lord, accepting the limitations imposed by tyrants.

Be happy that God has chosen you to bear His image in your soul. It is a free gift. Be thankful for it. And cease to judge yourselves and others.

The Sasover rabbi once gave his last coin to a man of evil reputation. His disciples asked him why he did so. He replied, "Should I be more particular in my choice than God, who gave the coin to me?" God has chosen you to be moulded in His likeness without any merit of yours. Now you also must love other men independently of their moral and spiritual status.

Yes, lieutenant, we—the ugly, haggard prisoners—bear His image. Amen.

CHAPTER 4

Hearing and Seeing

DEAR BROTHERS AND SISTERS,

The central message of the Mosaic law begins with the word "hear"—"Hear, O Israel: The Lord our God, the Lord is one!" (Deuteronomy 6:4). There were exceptional personalities in the Jewish religion who saw—men such as Moses and Isaiah. But the people had to hear, and to obey what they heard.

Christ said to His first disciples, "Come and *see*" (John 1:39). We have passed from hearing to seeing. To Martha, the Lord said, "Did I not say to you that if you would believe you would *see* the glory of God?" (John 11:40). The Book of Revelation, too, is a book about things that John actually *saw*.

The highest Jewish spiritual exercise is meditation on the Word. The Christians know a higher stage: contemplation. They can visualize.

In conditions of solitary confinement, which are similar to those of a hermit in the desert deprived of material things, the seeing becomes so real that you have difficulty convincing yourself that what you see is an event in the spirit and not in the material world.

This reminds me of two old Chinese legends. How true legends can be. It is said that a great painter once painted on a wall a beautiful landscape with a cave. When he had finished, he walked into the cave and disappeared, and was never heard of again.

Another legend tells of an artist who painted a lake with reeds. Among the reeds he placed a fish. The painted fish swam in the lake, alive and happy like all fishes.

Whatever you create or evoke in the spirit can become a reality into which you can enter, and live, and disappear.

All I have in my cell is a bed with a straw mattress and a blanket. In the corner is a bucket. My only other possession is a tin mug. With no earthly possessions to live on, I live in the world of the promises of God. Faith sees them as already fulfilled.

"To him who overcomes I will give to eat from the tree of life, which is in the midst of the Paradise of God" (Revelation 2:7). Under the Nazis, I once had a narrow escape from death. Still under emotional stress, I told the story to a wise old pastor. When I had finished, he said, "If you have gone through all that, you had better eat." And he asked his wife to bring me some fish. So Jesus, when we meet Him and tell Him all the tribulations through which we have passed, will say, "Then let us first eat." I see Him leading me to the tree of life, which is simply life itself. A blind man whom He healed saw men who looked like trees. That is what we are really like. Our lives are "the tree that yields fruit according to its kind, whose seed is in itself" (Genesis 1:11). Now I lie down in the shadow of the tree of life. He plucks the fruit of everything good which I have done. I see Him bending over me and giving me to eat. It is written, not that we shall eat, but that we shall be given to eat. I am a beloved bride, and the Bridegroom cherishes me. He plucks the fruit for me, and puts it in my mouth.

What a man sows, that he will reap (Galatians 6:7). He enjoys now, for eternity, the fruits of his life of faith.

"To him who overcomes I will give some of the hidden manna to eat" (Revelation 2:17). *Manna* means "What is this?" —the words the Jews said not only in the wilderness, but also when they saw the Lord driving out an unclean spirit in the synagogue at Capernaum. It is an expression of amazement. I see so many amazing things in heaven. God has surprises for His children. There are many more joys here than I expected, and a greater capacity for enjoying many pleasures at the same time. In Indian art, Krishna is depicted with many arms. This is a basic archetype of the human soul. You need many arms in a world where you have so much to receive. Most of the beings around me are like this. So I feel the greater pity for a few others whom I see around me in heaven. They have their share of joy. But I find it tragic that they should be in heaven with one single arm. They have obeyed Jesus and cut off the hand that offended them. It would have been simpler to readjust their whole life so as to prevent their hand from offending.

I would not dare to say whom I have seen in paradise. No one would believe me. This much I can say, that it contains more people than the average Christian would permit to enter.

I see something like an Orthodox church—that is the nearest comparison I can make, but it is something completely different. In it I see among the worshipers an exclusive brother, who would never have entered an Orthodox church during his earthly life. I ask him, "How do you come to be here?" He answers, "In heaven, there are many mansions. We, the exclusive brethren, have our own quite separate dwelling. But we enjoy visiting each other."

"And I will give him," says the Lord, "a white stone" (Revelation 2:17). I have actually received it. "And on the stone a new name written."

The Communists have put me in jail under the false name of Vasile Georgescu. I have been forbidden to reveal to anyone my true identity. They are afraid that a warden may commit an indiscretion. But it is not only they who give new names. God also gives new names. God was not satisfied with the name of Abram. He wished that its pronunciation should last longer, so he added a syllable to it. We would never have thought that God would appear to a man just to give him a nicer, more meaningful name. But, not satisfied with this, God changed Sarai's name, too. He called her Sarah, because that is the Hebrew name for "princess." She was a princess in His sight. Jesus changed Simon's name to

Cephas (John 1:42), a simplified form of Caiaphas (the high priest of that time), to show him that he, the ignorant fisherman, was the real high priest in the Lord's sight, and not the man who dressed in gorgeous robes.

I also received from Christ a new name. After something like a year, it was changed. It was not only that I heard it, I saw His face, the movements of His lips when He pronounced it. And the name lost its importance for me. Before He pronounced it there had been His desire to give it to me. The name was new only as applied to me. It was a biblical name. There was in His mind a comparison between me and the persons who have borne it before. There was the ineffable source out of which His thoughts have their provenance. I had touched the depths. The new name was only a hint inviting me to these depths.

When Jesus breathed upon the apostles and said, "Receive the Holy Spirit" (John 20:22), they surely caught His quiet breathing rather than the words He said while expelling the air. It is in catching this quiet breathing that you receive the Holy Spirit.

"And he who overcomes, and keeps My works until the end, to him I will give power over the nations" (Revelation 2:26). I see myself on a throne. Why should a throne be made of gold and velvet? Can it not as well be the few planks of a prisoner's bed? Men have given a certain kind of chair the name of "throne." I can give this name to any other object I please. From this my throne I decide about nations.

If Christians have the monopoly of salvation, over whom will they rule? And how will this promise be fulfilled, that to faithful servants is given the authority over five or ten cities (Luke 19:17–19)? It is no fun to be king over empty towns. So they will be populated by those who have not been faithful servants. We Christians will be in the heavenly Jerusalem, but there will also be nations walking in its light (Revelation 21:24). The leaves of the tree of life will serve for the healing of the nations (Revelation 22:2), which means that there will be in the life beyond people who need a cure for their souls.

And I am seated on a throne, and have the power to do good to multitudes of people. I can send messengers to give light and health. I get reports about the progress of difficult cases. They have to be thought about. There is no rest in heaven. It is the busiest place I know.

I see myself clothed in white garments (Revelation 3:5). I read this promise to Mihai when he was small. He was worried, "But what if the Lord does not have clothes small enough for children like me?" I had to assure him that Jesus has white garments of every size, for giants and dwarfs and children. He also has white garments for those who are small in faith as well as in body. Even the apostle Peter was once chastised by Jesus, "O you of little faith" (Matthew 14:31). A little dog may be despised by a big Doberman, but the Doberman has to recognize that the little dog is also a dog, and not a cat.

> Jesus has white garments of every size, for giants and dwarfs and children.

I am dressed in white, in fullness of light, and so are all those around me. We walk with Jesus. What a privilege it was to walk with Him through the earthly meadows! Birds sang more melodiously than ever. Lilies bloomed with a scent never smelled before. But we walk with Him in the golden streets of the heavenly city.

An old Jewish book, *Sefer Ierahmeel*, says that in the life to come the day is divided into four watches. In the first watch, we shall be like children, and shall know all the joys of childhood. In the second watch we shall be young, and know all the joys of youth. In the third watch we shall know all the joys of maturity, and in the fourth watch those of the wisdom of old age. Next day, the cycle of joys begins again. It really is so. I pass from joy to joy.

Like the Chinese painter, I enter this cave, painted once by the apostle John and now once more by me. Like the painted fish I swim in the water. No man can become a future citizen of heaven without passing hours in heaven now. Therefore we have been given the power to ascend in the spirit. Poverty, sickness, inner and outer tragedies, prisons, or chains cannot hinder this ascent. On the contrary, they assist it.

Oh my brothers and sisters, why remain in the ugly places? Evoke heaven and enter forever into what you have evoked.

What will death matter then?

The Zohar, an ancient book of Jewish mysticism, says, "When such a soul departs from this world, pure, bright, unblemished, the Holy One, blessed be he, daily causes her to shine with a host of radiances, and proclaims concerning her, 'Here is the soul of my son such a one. Let her be preserved for the body from which she has departed.'"

Just as "Jacob kissed Rachel" (Genesis 29:11), the Lord discerns each holy soul and, taking each in turn, embraces and caresses her. To die is to pass into His embrace. Amen.

CHAPTER 5

The Pain of the Imagination

DEAR BROTHERS AND SISTERS,

I don't know what is happening to me now.

The tuberculosis microbe has invaded my whole body. I spit blood. On the spots where I was most severely beaten, bone tuberculosis has fixed itself. I have read somewhere that the secretion of the tuberculosis microbe greatly excites certain glands, giving rise to rich erotic imagery.

It may be that they put aphrodisiacs in our food. A pastor in a nearby cell was forced to sleep in the same bed as a girl prisoner, only to torment them both.

The fact is, it is a battle to defend myself against such fantasy. You young people, when you have it, can escape by reading a book, listening to music, or taking a walk. I lie on my bed and imagine, for hours at a time, all kinds of wild scenes in which I myself am taking part. There is nothing here to help me redirect my imagination.

I cannot escape from this torture into any other activity. And I feel a deep disgust with myself for having impure thoughts about women who were my former parishioners—some of them won for Christ by me.

But we have to bear such crosses, too. There is an objective law of the soul, just as in the material world. Given a man of a certain type, under such circumstances, such thoughts are a natural result. We can try to do our best, even when we are haunted by obscene imagination.

Here you are, Helen, tempting me.

Your name reminds me of many things. One beautiful Helen was the cause of the Trojan war in which so many heroes died. There must be a value in a beautiful Helen.

At the beginning of the fourth century, Christians were thrown to the wild beasts under the Emperor Diocletian. A Christian servant at the court of Queen Helen brought her to salvation. The Queen persuaded her son, Constantine the Great, to free the Christians. That was the beginning of our Christian civilization. So much can a Helen achieve! It was because of his wife, Helen, that the name of Constantius and their more famous son, Constantine, entered history.

And what if, under the influence of drugs, or simply because of long sexual abstinence, I see you in provocative poses now my dear Helen? Does it diminish anything of your value?

What a fight I had to win you for Christ! You belonged to a family with Communist affiliations, and refused to come to church. You said once, "If Pastor Wurmbrand wishes me to become a Christian, he will have to come every Sunday evening and repeat the whole sermon just for me." So I did, Sunday after Sunday. I came even when I was very tired. I came on cold winter evenings. I came once even when I had a fever.

Usually, priests and pastors do not have to fight for souls. A Catholic couple have a child who is born destined to be the Catholic priest's parishioner. When the child is brought to baptism, the priest has one more member in his church without any battle. The same kind of thing happens in Protestant denominations. When you don't have to fight for souls, you don't value them as much. You don't love them as much. Not every pastor weeps when he loses them, or seeks them when they go astray.

I have fought for you, Helens and Marias and Floricas. You were my every day's work and my every night's prayer. Why should I wonder that you are now the objects of my obsessions?

As my mind and memory are increasingly deteriorating under

the influence of drugs and hunger, these erotic imageries may be the manner in which God is reminding me of you, and of every one of those souls who, left without their pastor, have a heavy battle to fight. Perhaps what appears to my conscience as a disgusting sexual obscenity is a distorted image of the uniting of our souls in the battle against the forces of evil.

You, Maria, had an only daughter sick with a heart disease. The girl begged not to have an operation, but you decided otherwise, and she submitted. She died under the anesthetic. After that you were heartbroken. My visits were a comfort to you.

An erotic fantasy reminded me of you. We don't see things as they are, so perhaps I don't see what is really happening now between us. What may seem to me to be an obscenity may be a false image, under the terrifying prison experience, of a beautiful reality, a holy union of our souls. It may be that it is a distorted image of our bending together over the soul of your daughter, Yvonne.

In Romans 8:28, Paul tells us, "All things work together for good to those who love God." St. Augustine adds, "even my sins." Perhaps these fantasies too.

And then, aren't we to share the sufferings of the Man of Sorrows? Were not the sorrows of all who are in pain His also? What about the pain of sexual desire which cannot find fulfillment? It is one of the great sufferings of mankind. So many beautiful souls cannot find a suitable partner; others are sick. With some, utter poverty or a wrong education is a hindrance. Many are unhappy because they have not been able to marry, or because they have married the wrong person. Sexual obsession is one of the great tragedies of mankind. Jesus' heart is open to this suffering also.

If He is in me, the suffering of the world is a burden which I must bear, too. God being in me, His responsibilities become mine. Jesus gave His disciples power to forgive sins and to retain them (John 20:23). But in order to use this power well, they also must be tempted in all things. There is an educational value in such things happening to me. God shapes His ministers.

There is value in all the sexual sufferings through which you pass, my brothers and sisters. They teach you to understand people, to love them as they are, to do your best to see that there should be more sexual justice, in the same way as a Christian has to work to bring about political and economic justice.

Jesus said that there will be a world in which people will not marry, nor be given in marriage (Matthew 22:30). If you pick flowers and put them in a vase, they become your property. You can uproot a plant and put it in a pot. It will be yours. But why not leave all the flowers to grow in the garden, so that all can enjoy together, without claim of property, their beauty and their perfume?

God will be all in all. Unfettered, we shall all meet in Him. There will be no one who is not in unity with everyone else, and everyone will be like Christ—splendid, radiant, full of virtue and perfection. Therefore we shall neither marry nor be given in marriage.

> If He is in me, the suffering of the world is a burden which I must bear, too.

These erotic images are only a cheap imitation. Perhaps they are a dim representation of heaven, when Richards and Georges and Stephens and Helens and Marias and Floricas, in glorified bodies, will live in a spiritual embrace of each other and of God, a life of increasing love in the spirit and in glorified bodies.

So let us remain serene, even through those tormenting imaginings from which, in a different measure, many of you also suffer. Christ is with us in these things, too.

The Communists have lost the battle of doping us with aphrodisiacs.

Rejoice, my young brothers and sisters. Christ conquers this temptation. Amen.

CHAPTER 6

Mary Sees Everything

DEAR BROTHERS AND SISTERS,

I have no books. I never speak to anyone. It has been quite a long time since I was last called to an interrogation. I live intellectually on the thoughts that flash through my mind. Sometimes I hear my thoughts.

A few days ago—it was on Good Friday—suddenly a voice said distinctly, "Mary sees everything." This was contrary to all I had previously thought about the mother of the Lord.

Since I had become a Christian, I had always held her in high respect. A woman does not become a Jewess by giving birth to a Jew. She gives birth to a Jew because she is a Jewess. And Mary did not become the mother of the Lord by giving birth to the Lord. She gave birth to him because she was essentially a God-bearer. This potential existed in her before her meeting with the archangel Gabriel. She said, "All generations will call me blessed" (Luke 1:48). And I have always called her the blessed virgin, though this is very unusual for a Protestant.

But I could not admit the practice of addressing prayers to her. In order to hear them, she would have to possess the divine attribute of omnipresence. She is not everywhere. She is a human being. She is merely a saint in glory, and they have their limitations. They are creatures, not the Creator.

I have often argued along these lines with my Orthodox and

Catholic friends. They seem to forget sometimes how unspeakably small Mary felt herself to be, and how unworthy, when she held the infant Jesus in her arms. They could do well to bear in mind what their own hymns say.

There is a beautiful hymn sung in the Orthodox churches every Good Friday, which expresses the awe Mary's Son inspired in her: "O Son, my Son, how shall I wrap thee in swaddling clothes? How shall I give thee milk, who givest food to all creation? How shall I hold thee in my arms, who holdest all things? How shall I look upon thee without fear, on whom the many-eyed cherubim dare not lift their gaze?"

And now, out of the unknown, comes this voice saying, "Mary sees everything." Strangely, far from being scandalized, the thought gives me comfort. For days, I have kept repeating to myself, "Mary sees everything." I feel so happy about it. I have not the slightest desire to pass on to any other thought. I am reminded of the story of a Jewish rabbi who was observed reading a page of the Bible. Hours later, he was seen still pondering over the same page. More hours passed. Still he had not turned the page. He was asked, "Why don't you read further?" and he answered, "This page is so beautiful. Why should I go on to the next?"

St. Francis prayed, *Dio mio e toto mio*—my God and my all." God was his all. To Mary, her holy Son was everything. I cannot always say that He is everything for me. I love many other things besides Him. To her, He was and is Everything. She sees only Him, she sees others only in Him, through Him, as if through His eyes.

One evening Joseph was cold toward her. She could guess that he wished to leave her because she was pregnant. But she saw no sin in his suspicion; she did not tell him what had happened. She did not defend herself. She looked toward her Everything and could be quiet. What did it matter if Joseph thought her impure?

The Lord greatly humbled Himself, and humility cannot be insulted. The friends of Jesus said, "He is out of His mind"

(Mark 3:21). Mary looked to her Lord and did not quarrel with those who insulted Him, knowing that He is above any insult. She never saw anyone other than the One who is her Everything.

The brothers of Jesus did not believe in Him (John 7:5). She did not tell them to believe. She trusted that they would. She did not even notice their disbelief. It was only transitory. Later, one of these brothers was to become an apostle and die a martyr's death.

She did not complain at the foot of the cross that the disciples had forsaken Him. After the resurrection, He did not show Himself to her. It was not necessary. She saw Him, the Everything, even when He was not before her eyes. Afterward she sat quietly in the midst of the church at Jerusalem, attending services conducted by an apostle who had fled in the dark, or by Peter who had denied his Master. She saw no sin in them.

As one who put her faith in the Lord, she was a partaker of the divine nature. She had the nature of One who does not observe iniquity in Jacob, nor wickedness in Israel (Numbers 23:21).

"God saw everything that He had made, and indeed it was very good" (Genesis 1:31). Everything is very good. Only if you look at things in isolation do they appear sometimes good and sometimes bad. *"Toto mio."* For Mary, Jesus was the Everything. Through him, everything she sees is good.

In Acts 22, we are told that, while Paul was in a trance in the temple, the Lord appeared to him with the practical purpose of telling him where to go next. But Paul, instead of talking business with Christ, reminded Him, "In every synagogue I imprisoned and beat those who believe on You. And when the blood of Your martyr Stephen was shed, I also was standing by consenting to his death" (Acts 22:19,20).

The Lord wished to speak with Paul about a beautiful future of service and self-sacrifice, crowned with martyrdom at the end. Paul answered by remembering the past.

The Lord refused even to talk to Paul on the subject, completely uninteresting for Him, of Paul's former misdeeds. When you speak in His presence about your past sins, He does not even understand your language. Only the present and the future have any interest for Him.

I have wasted so much time in my solitary cell remembering my past. I was a very bad child. At the age of six I threw a knife at my mother, showing criminal tendencies. By the time I was fifteen, I was already something worse than my present jailers. They at least have some kind of discipline. I was on a lower level than they. I was, and remained until my conversion, an anarchic element, capable of any misdeed, for or against the revolutionist cause. I hated God, mocked Him publicly, and tried to persuade everyone else to hate Him. If I loved Marx and Bakunin and Kropotkin, it was not for their political or economic doctrines, but chiefly for their antitheism. I have committed crimes and have blood on my conscience. I told Jesus about it again and again. But because He had long ago washed all this away, there was no possibility of communication between us. He did not understand what I was talking about.

God had separated Paul from his mother's womb. He chose me, too, before the foundation of the world. It would have been a curious kind of election if He had not foreordained all my steps. My sins belonged to His mysterious plans. God tried to make something whiter than snow. The only raw material out of which He can achieve such whiteness is grave sin of which a man repents. There is a deep significance in falling into sin. The Book of Daniel says, "Some of those of understanding shall fall, to refine them, purge them, and make them white" (Daniel 11:35).

Past sins, if you repent of them, whiten you. They made a great psalmist out of David, a faithful believer out of the prostitute Rahab, a zealous apostle out of the persecutor Saul. I have been a loved preacher and writer with a particular vocation. My sermons and books would not have had the same quality without my past of anarchy, vice, and violent atheism.

When Paul touched on the problem of his past sins, the Lord did not react at all. He continued to give directions of the future. It was as if Paul had said nothing. And you really are speak-

41

ing about nothing when you speak about your past offenses. Where are they? They have as much reality as the snow of ten years ago. The statutes and judgments of God are given so that men shall live by them, and not that they may torture themselves slowly to death with continual remorse.

Jesus does not see any sin in me; it has all been washed away. He is God. Seeing the whole picture, He never rebukes, but only understands, only loves, only helps. So it is with those believers, like Mary, who make Jesus their focus—their Everything—and see as He sees.

> Jesus does not see any sin in me; it has all been washed away.

I promise—and oh, Lord, help me to keep the promise when provoked to do otherwise—never to mention my past sins, neither before You nor before men. In the frame of eternity, they were preparatory steps toward holiness. For saints, past sins have formed the roots of future beautiful flowers. I will live only the present and the future, learning from Mary not to see meaningless isolated fragments, but the great, beautiful Everything.

Hail, Mary, who sees Everything. Amen.

CHAPTER 7

The Remnant of My Faith

DEAR BROTHERS AND SISTERS,

A faith that can be destroyed by suffering is not faith.

I have read many stories of men who experienced great sorrows, but who believed to the end; stories of martyrs, and of missionary heroes. Bishop Hannington of Uganda must have preached to the cannibals about a faith that endures through every suffering. Then they took him away to be eaten. On the way to the place where they cut his body into pieces, he repeated to himself all the time, "Love your enemies,...pray for those who spitefully use you" (Matthew 5:44). When his sons took his place as missionaries and converted the bishop's murderers, they were told the story. So he must have kept his faith unaltered to the end. A man will continue to hold his true creed even in the face of death. You give up only what you imagined you believed.

Today I have had a time of quiet to think about what I have really retained of the creed I used to hold.

The relationship between the body and the soul is a curious one. The soul does not always seem to be tied to the body. When I was arrested, for weeks it was as if my soul had remained at home. This lasted for quite a time, until my soul accepted the new situation, joined my body, and began to function normally as the soul of a prisoner. The Orthodox say that for forty days after death, the soul of the dead man remains near his old home with those he has loved. Only after this—a period equal to that for which Jesus remained on earth after His resurrection—does the soul go to its destination.

Is there something in this? Perhaps the soul does not immediately follow the body. After a session of heavy torture, my soul is not in my cell, but remains, obsessed by what it has endured, in the place of torture. The torturers are no longer there. They are no longer concerned with me. But I live over and over again the past tortures, until they become infinitely multiplied.

Now my soul has come back to me; I scarcely have any more pain. I can think quietly about my faith.

Certainly I believe that God is the maker of heaven and earth. I could not explain the existence of the universe otherwise. This is called theism. But it is unimportant to me how this universe came to be. God made it. Fine. Reason is satisfied with this. But what about the rest?

My reason categorically refuses to believe that God is love. Your interrogators tie you to a chair. Your head has been shaved, and at intervals of one minute, tup-tup-tup, a drop of water falls on you, always in the same spot. And this happens in a world ruled by the God of love! Martin Luther called reason a beast because it gave him arguments against the faith. But I treat it as a beast when it puts forward arguments to convince me that belief is the right thing. Reason tells me that I have free will and that I, and others, have chosen to sin. Hence all sorrows! Suffering is the unavoidable outcome of sin. (Something unavoidable in the universe of an almighty God! It makes me laugh!) But why then do babies suffer? What have they done to deserve it?

Men are torn to pieces by wild animals; poisoned by reptiles; killed by microbes and viruses. Do they deserve it? How is it that the God of love had prepared the viruses long ages beforehand, against the eventuality that man would sin? And again I ask, why do babies die? Because of the sin of Adam and Eve. But did death exist in nature before the Fall? God said to Adam, "Of the tree of the knowledge of good and evil you shall not eat, for in the day that you eat of it you shall surely die" (Genesis 2:17).

If Adam had not known the phenomenon of death, these words would have been completely unintelligible to him. Perhaps he knew what "death" meant. Eve, too, might have understood it, when the serpent assured her that she would not die. Perhaps she had seen animals dying. Death is the wages of sin for men, but why would animals die even in paradise? Why do fishes and crabs suffer in the depths of the sea? They have never even seen a man. To the lost world, it is madness to believe that fishes eat one another because a man has sinned.

I shudder every time I say the word "madness." I see that it is the unavoidable outcome for me. (Again something unavoidable in an almighty God's universe.) I fight against madness, and cling desperately to reason. Why did Luther not cling to reason? Why did he call it a beast? He too knew maddening suffering. Sometimes he actually raged like a madman.

He, seeing himself driven towards madness, simply threw himself trustingly into its arms.

The whole story of a God of love is madness. It is madness that God should love, not only the good people, but also those who use the Chinese drip torture and make jokes while you suffer. And how can He love the dictator who sits quietly in his office and never touches anybody himself, but orders these things to happen? Equally mad is the story of redemption by the blood of Christ. My reason rejects it. And if I don't keep my reason, the purpose of the Communists will have been attained. I shall begin to yell, and to bang on the door. I shall be put in a straitjacket and shall end up in an asylum.

But could I not be mad in a reasonable way—reasonably mad? In the conflict between Galileo and his inquisitors, reason was on the side of the inquisitors. It was obvious, a simple fact proved by the senses since humanity existed, that the sun moves around the earth. Galileo's assertion was mad. But observations, experiments, and calculations were made, and what was madness became reasonable. Galileo was reasonably mad. It is reasonably mad to believe that I am surrounded not by strong walls, but only by whirlwinds of electrons, with huge spaces between them.

And if the earth is in fact circling madly without any reason for doing so, and all this time has been mocking our senses, if elementary particles are dancing around as unpredictably as madmen, then the ultimate truth in religion is obtained in a very strange biblical expression. While all other religious writings flatter God and speak of Him in the most reverent language, the Bible speaks of "the foolishness of God" (1 Corinthians 1:25). Maybe He does love, but not as a reasonable being would. He loves to the point of folly, in the truest sense of that word. The Chinese drip cannot come from the love of a reasonable God. But it might have a place in the plan of a God's foolishness, or it might be an expression of the weakness of a deeply loving God. Paul speaks in the same verse about both the foolishness and the weakness of God. If God is almighty, He must also have a capacity for weakness and madness. Nothing is impossible for Him, not even this.

We think of Job and David as holy men, but they both said the most blasphemous things about God. Even Jesus, on the cross, accused a God whom He had proclaimed as love of forsaking His only begotten Son in His sufferings. Whatever the motive, this is surely not a very laudable attitude for a God. At one time I used to prostrate myself before God. But to reproach God with a lack of love, or at least a lack of normal love, is also a part of religion.

Othello loved, and killed because he loved. Was this not love? Desdemona accepted it as such and, in her turn, loved to the end the one who strangled her. That madman had the right wife. Job displayed the same spirit when he said, "Though He slay me, yet will I trust Him" (Job 13:15).

There is a foolishness in God, and a corresponding foolishness in the saints. My reason stops short at theism. But Einstein demanded that we relinquish convictions which we have held for so long that they have become synonymous with common sense. I will give up common sense in religion, too. If Einstein consigned to the flames the classic laws of physics, we must do the same with the classic notion of love. God loves in a sense of this word which is different from our use of it. And, as for me, my foolish love will not stop where my reason stops. God loved us without any deserving on our part. I will love Him, and believe in Him and in His plan of redemption, without any reasonable cause, simply because it pleases Him.

And having once given up reason, I will go all the way with madness. I will love my torturers, too, though to do so is sheer folly. And when you, Jesus, come to take us to Yourself, I will make it difficult for You. I will refuse to go with You. I will keep my arms firmly around the worst of hangmen, and I will say to You, "I go to heaven only if he comes too." You will have to yield.

> "Despise the devil. The devil is a proud spirit. He cannot endure to be mocked."

As for you, Devil, I recognize you now. It was you who made me doubt.

In the early days of my Christian faith, I was very much assaulted by a certain temptation. I asked an Armenian Catholic priest, a very wise man, what I should do about it. He answered, "Despise the devil." Thomas More said, "The devil is a proud spirit. He cannot endure to be mocked."

Later, I found the same thought in Luther: the best way to drive out the devil, if he will not yield to texts of Scripture, is to jeer and flout him, because he cannot bear scorn.

Stupid devil, he hopes to wipe out my faith with the arguments of reason. But arguments are not so painful as beatings and the Chinese drip. If these have not destroyed my faith, should I abandon it because the battered reason of my little mind finds fault with it? I renounce you, reason, and the devil who inspires you, and I will remain madly attached to the foolishness of God which is wiser than men, and to His weakness which is stronger than men. Amen.

CHAPTER 8

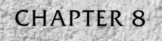

MOTHER,

Jesus has led me at last to still waters.

The period of instruction of my case is finished. Soon I shall appear before the court. I did not defend myself before the examining officers. I shall not defend myself before the judges. Lao-Tse rightly said, "Those who justify themselves do not convince." I signed everything they asked me to sign against myself. I refused only to accuse others.

Why should I justify myself before the Communists? I am sure I am right in my attitude toward them. But you cannot be right without being wrong at the same time. "Fair is foul, and foul is fair," say the witches in *Macbeth*. To believe that you can be entirely right without also being wrong is like believing you have a front without a back. Because I hate communism, the Communists must defend themselves against me, as I defend the cause of the Church against them.

The chapter of instruction, with its torture, is finished.

The waters have become still in my relationship with God also. Things have taken on a crystalline clarity. A god from whom I can depart, who would let me go, who would not keep me to the end, never was a god. I can rest completely tranquil. The real God will uphold me.

I have passed through the period of remorse for past sins,

and the period of moral perplexities over lying or not lying at interrogations. I know the evil in me, and I know the good. I can use both. The Lord has said, "You shall love the Lord your God with all your heart" (Deuteronomy 6:5). How can a man love God with all his heart, if in the heart there are so many wicked passions?

When we were children, we used to play on the seashore throwing a ball from one to the other. The ball floated both on the crests and in the troughs of the waves. So does the faithful soul, until it ceases to judge itself. There are no such things as good flowers and bad flowers. There are simply flowers. One is a tulip, another a rose, another a violet. Some have a fragrance, some do not. Some are gorgeously colored. Others are modest. So our souls are as God has created them. Some mountains are high, but you do not have to be an Everest to be called a mountain; neither do you have to be a hero of faith in order to be a Christian.

I try not to compare myself with anyone. I am what I am, and in this knowledge I lie down in green pastures. I no longer live between two states of existence, my past liberty and a future reunion with those I love. I am able to realize the kingdom of God present within me at this moment.

I knew very little of Father; he died when I was nine. He was a very taciturn man. I don't remember ever having heard him speak. He only gave me a deep look. I went to see him in the hospital the morning he died. Even then he told me nothing. He had heard the gospel. Probably he could not communicate in words what he knew. He was silent. (The New Testament never mentions a word ever spoken by Joseph.) That very afternoon, I went to meet you, Mother, when you returned from the hospital. You were in tears and said, "From now on you will be orphans." I remember weeping. Then followed the burial, a simple ceremony for a poor man. The coffin was made of a few planks, not even painted black. An old Jew with a beard and side-curls said the prayer, *"El mole rahamim*—God full of mercy." None of us understood then what he was singing. We came home. You fainted. Father came into my mind no more, until now.

Thirty years have passed. During the night, I feel his presence in my cell. I have his image before my eyes. He is silent, as he always was. Only his eyes speak. And his eyes make me understand why the Lord said to Peter after he had sinned, "Simon, son of Jonah, do you love Me?" (John 21:16). Why did He remind Peter just at that moment, and only at that moment, about his father? Because we grieve our parents terribly when we sin. We are pleasing to them when we walk in the ways of righteousness. I could see no approval on my father's face, nor rebuke. He was waiting to see the outcome of the struggle.

I did not know my father, but you, Mother, I knew. How I regret that I was a bad son.

When I was small, I would turn the handle of the sewing-machine for you as you sewed. You would sing to me, always the same two songs. One was about a monk who, being asked what had driven him to the monastic life, answered, "Two blue eyes." When I saw those two blue eyes which look into the ultimate depths of the soul, and became a Christian, you did not understand it. I read to you one evening the story of Christ's death and resurrection. You wept over it. You never spoke about it afterward. I remember your second song was "Silent Night." Where did you, a Jewess, pick it up? And why were you always singing it?

It was a deadly blow for you when I experienced my silent night, and Jesus was born in my heart.

Where are you now, Mother? Are you weeping?

In a cell near me there seems to be an elderly woman. Her daughter must also be a prisoner. When she is led past a certain cell, the mother begins to cry, "Ioana, Ioana," and begs the guards to allow her to see her child. She says, "I will kiss your hands with which you have beaten my daughter, if only I can see her." The guards laugh, "We would rather have her kisses than yours," and they pass by.

And then the mother yells and bangs her fists on the door.

Afterward she becomes silent. Perhaps they have gagged her. Perhaps they have given her an injection.

How was it with Mary when her Son was led away to His death? "Rachel weeping for her children, refusing to be comforted" (Matthew 2:18). Did anyone comfort you, mother of the Lord, for so much suffering of your Son's disciples?

Most of your statues in churches do not correspond to the picture I have of you. In the statues you are shown very much like a nun, with a rosary in your hand. You are smiling serenely. But nuns have no children. You have. Your true likeness has yet to be depicted.

Foolish, foolish thoughts—it has been a long time since I had a normal one. The apostle John saw a woman clothed with the sun and with the moon under her feet, and upon her head a crown of twelve stars (Revelation 12:1). Representing believers throughout the ages, she is beyond bowing to a Communist.

But how about you, Mama? Will you be able to come to see your Richard, your youngest son, again?

I remember your heroism and self-sacrifice. Left a widow with four small children, you brought us up to adulthood. I remember you in all your beauty. You were in your seventies when they arrested me. But you still had a brilliant and youthful appearance, with hardly any wrinkles.

Will age have made your beauty decay? Will you die, and have passed away forever, and will we never meet again? You are not a Christian. St. Thomas Aquinas said that one of the joys of heaven will be to see the endless tortures of the damned in hell. A cannibal could not have said it better. I don't believe it. When I first went into a church, it seemed to me to have wings. Would the Church's wings not be strong enough to carry you, too, to heaven? The Communists mock the mother near me. But they cannot mock my feelings, my love toward you.

I pray that you will be saved, Mama. Then you will have your silent night in heaven. You will look into those two blue eyes and will leave everything for them, as the monk did about whom you sang.

When Jesus tells me, "Well done," He will call me "Richard, son of Henric and Amalia," as He said "Simon, son of Jonas," when Peter sinned. And if Richard, son of Henric and Amalia, is to inherit the kingdom, he will not want his parents to remain outside it.

A parable tells of a young man who loved a girl to folly. One evening he could stand it no more. He knocked at her door and begged, "Let me in. I must be with you." She asked, "But who is it?" He answered, "It is I, your beloved," to which she replied, "My room is narrow and my bed is straight. There is no place for you." He left and wandered for years through the world, not understanding her refusal. He had assumed that she loved him, too. But the moment of enlightenment came. He knocked at her door again. She asked, "Who is it?" He answered, "It is you." The door opened for him. He was received with embraces. She said, "For years I have waited for this moment."

> I pray that you will be saved, Mama. Then you will have your silent night in heaven.

Heaven, Mama, is a narrow place. There is room in it only for one. The soul who wishes to enter must be able to say at the gate, "It is You, Christ."

This will be difficult for you, Mama. You have not known him. But say, "It is Richard's mother," and Jesus will lovingly receive you when you come to Him. David asked, "Is there still anyone who is left of the house of Saul, that I may show him kindness for Jonathan's sake?" (2 Samuel 9:1), and he was good to a worthless man, Mephibosheth, for his friend's sake. Jesus calls me His friend. He is more generous than David. I desire that all of my house be saved, and you belong to it. So does Father. So does my little sister Mary, for whom I long so much. I have never seen her. She died before I was born. But in this cell I have a burning desire to be with her. If we shall all be together, it will no longer be the Richard who often made you weep. Everything will be new.

Don't cry, Mama. Goodnight. I pray we see each other again.

Angels, you, too, must obey what is written. The Scriptures say that, "when He is revealed, we shall be like Him" (1 John 3:2). He is with His mother. I wish to be like Him in this respect also. See to it, angels. Amen.

CHAPTER 9

Imprecise Thought

BELOVED CONGREGATION,

Every day I tell myself at least one new joke. The one for today was this: A man was complaining to his friend about doctors. "They write so illegibly. Don't you think there should be a law obliging them to write so that everyone can read it?" "No," answered his friend. "God forbid. I have a completely illegible prescription from a doctor. With it I have passed through several customs offices without any trouble. I have traveled free on trains and I have even been exempted from taxes."

I laughed dutifully. Then I thought, so many people complain that the Bible is full of contradictions and mysterious, incomprehensible passages. Is there not a good purpose in this? Is it not just for this reason that for so many centuries men of all kinds of religious beliefs and of different intellectual caliber—slave owners and slaves, feudal lords and revolutionaries, socialists and capitalists, schoolchildren and eminent scientists—have all passed unhindered through the customs offices of life with the Bible as their guide? The fact is that Hebrew and Greek are full of double meanings, and capable of many different legitimate translations. Is there any value in imprecision, in vagueness?

My first impulse would be to deny it.

There is only one thing I hate more than communism, and that is lack of precision in thinking.

Every false, every imprecise thought makes the very operation of thinking appear unreliable. And as a result men are driven to irrational actions that have not been properly thought out. Imprecise thought drives them to drugs, alcohol, and other excesses —all means of evading reason, which apparently gives false results.

As a matter of fact, even the reason I hate communism is not so much because of its brutality as because of its imprecise thinking. A good musician feels something like a physical pain when the orchestra plays a false chord. In the same way it makes my heart ache when I hear thoughts expressed that are not logically precise.

It is said that a radical agitator once rode his bicycle to Hyde Park in London, where he left the bicycle against a fence as he addressed the crowd. "Property is theft," he said. "We are all descended from Adam and Eve, or from a pair of monkeys. At the beginning there were no rich and poor. How is it that some are rich now? They have stolen from their neighbors. By taking from rich men you are taking from expropriators. To take back what has been stolen from you is not theft. So if you need anything, you are entitled simply to take it. No policeman in the world has the authority to stop you. Everything belongs to everyone." The crowd applauded him. But when he wanted to go home, his bicycle was missing. He at once began to shout, "Police! Police! My bicycle has been stolen!"

Communists think wrongly, which is a greater crime than brutality. It is a sin against reason.

But there are certain ambiguous and mysterious matters about which our thinking becomes more precise as it becomes more imprecise. In such matters the object of thought has no precision in itself. A system is projected into it, from my mind, and this falsifies reality. Every definition of the Godhead, of the kingdom, of eternal life, must be false. We have to do here with mysteries. The God of love and the God of revenge, both the same God, is an ambiguous God. Only ambiguous thinking can reflect His reality. He is a mystery, and we think rightly about Him in the mystery and confusion of the subconscious rather than in the clear-cut definitions of the scholars.

Let us not allow ourselves to be led astray by the plainness of biblical statements such as "God is love" (1 John 4:8). When David Livingstone first went to the primitive tribes of Central Africa, he could not preach to them about this verse, because their language did not have the word "love." So he asked them, "What is the thing you like best?" They answered, *"Unboi.* It is the name we give to meat from the arm of a man after it has been smoked. There is nothing better in the world than *unboi."* Then Livingstone delivered his famous sermon on the theme that "God is the best *unboi,"* and with this he reached the hearts of the primitive people. You may think it blasphemy to compare God with pastrami from the arm of a man. But did not John do something similar when he said that "God is love"? Love is a human affection toward a person we strongly like. The higher animals also know this affection. Does anybody believe that God is an affection shared by men and animals? But love was the highest thing known to the Jewish and Greek contemporaries of the apostle, just as *unboi* was the highest thing known to the African cannibal. So John said that God is love. As for God, He is what He is, neither pastrami nor an emotion. He is a mystery that cannot be put into words. A person who thinks about Him in precise terms is imprecise in his thinking. Only vagueness is precise in this sphere. My Christianity is undogmatic. Dogmas are much too clear-cut.

When my son, Mihai, was small, his favorite books in the Bible were Nehemiah (which he pronounced "Nehembiah") and the Book of Revelation; the first because Nehemiah not only struck some whom he disliked, but also pulled out their hair (Nehemiah 13:25). (I had to explain to him in detail how this happened, whether he plucked out the hairs one by one or in handfuls.) The second he liked because of the multitude of beasts, dragons, and four-headed creatures.

His preferences compelled me to read Nehemiah over and over again. I remember it quite well. Nehemiah calls the Creator "the great, the mighty, and awesome God" (Nehemiah 9:32).

In the Babylonian Talmud, Rabbi Mathana says of this verse that he learned from Rabbi Jehoshua ben Levi that the scribes of the time of the second temple were called "men of the great synod" because they restored sovereignty to its rightful owner. Moses had said "the great God, mighty and awesome" (Deuteronomy 10:17). Then came Jeremiah, who must have thought, "The Gentiles are pillaging the temple. What has become of God's awesome nature?" So, in his prayer (Jeremiah 32:18), he leaves out the word "awesome." Later, Daniel said, "The Gentiles oppress His children. Where is His might?" Therefore, in his prayer (Daniel 9:4), he leaves out "the mighty." Then came the men of the great synod, who said, "On the contrary, this is His might, that He has power over His indignation and is longsuffering toward offenders. By this He shows that He is awesome, because if the Holy One, blessed be His name, were not so, how could our nation exist among the peoples of the world?"

God is mighty and awesome in His own way. Words applied to Him do not have the same meaning as when they are applied to us. He has the might to forget about Himself and to give His only begotten Son to help some infinitesimal beings who are in deadly danger. What man would use his might to help an ant to get out of trouble? God is mighty in an absolutely unique sense of this word.

We continue to sin even after we have become children of God. We sin before His very eyes. And He looks away from our offenses, keeping always the sweet remembrance of the moment of our conversion. Call this attribute of God his awesomeness if you like. But it is an awesomeness apart, without comparison.

How awesome is a God who strips Himself naked, because Roman soldiers armed with whips order Him to do so! He stripped Himself not only of His clothes, but also of His ability to perform miracles. He stripped His immaculate human nature of its immortality. This God cannot be put into words. We can only be changed into His likeness. Then people, looking at us, will believe in this strange God.

During an interrogation, a Christian was asked by a Communist officer, "Where is your God? Why doesn't He perform a miracle?" Our brother answered, "You have a great miracle before your eyes, but you are blind. You mock me and beat me. I look at you with love. That is the miracle."

We have to speak like this to the Communists. It may even convert them. We ourselves are not satisfied. We would like to see quite another miracle: that there should be no more beatings, no more suffering. But God is what He is, not what we want Him to be. This is why we call the Beloved awesome.

> "You mock me
>
> and beat me.
>
> I look at you
>
> with love. That
>
> is the miracle."

I have said that my Christianity is undogmatic. Again I use a human word, and it may mislead. Christianity can no more do without dogmas than natural sciences can do without laws.

But in many sciences the notion of the "natural law" has changed. Science has ceased to be consequent. The atom is considered, according to the needs of a given experiment, as a particle or as a wave. Nobody has seen it, and it cannot be located. So it makes no difference. Or try to imagine what geometry calls a point—an entity without dimension. It is impossible. Or, take Max Planck. He says that matter *per se* does not exist. Matter appears and remains only thanks to an energy which brings particles of the atom into orbit. This energy is the ultimate basis of matter.

This means that the scientist must live in different spheres. He has an object in his house that he can handle and sit on, which he calls a chair. When he begins to think about it in his laboratory, he knows it to be a whirlwind of elementary particles. When he draws philosophical conclusions from his science, the chair becomes an unreal object. Planck says that it is not the seen, transitory matter which is the real, the true, the existent, but the unseen, the immortal spirit, without which matter would not even exist. And having said this, he sits down on a chair with full confidence. On a practical level, he knows it to be matter.

So we have to live our life with God on different levels. There is practical religion, in which God is very like a man. He has eyes with which He looks on us. He can stretch out His arm to help us. He speaks to us in our language. He enjoys our songs and prayers.

When we meditate about Him, all these things disappear. No human words exist to explain Him. The French say, *"Un dieu defini est un dieu fini*—a god who is defined is a god who is finished." You cannot define His image.

Yes, we have a dogmatic Christianity, but its dogmas are inconsequent, vague, contradictory. God is light. Physicists will tell you that light behaves in an inconsequent, contradictory manner.

Imprecision is the only precise manner of thinking about God and His rules. The leap of faith is a leap into the vague, the indefinite, the equivocal, the uncertain, the undetermined.

"He hangs the earth on nothing" (Job 26:7). Hang your faith on nothing. Jesus "offered up prayers and supplications, with vehement cries and tears to Him who was able to save Him from death" (Hebrews 5:7). But He was not saved. He had to endure death. And on the cross He asked in vain, "My God, My God, why have You forsaken Me?" (Matthew 27:46). There came no answer and no help, but only a new mockery. To this mysterious, awesome God He said, "Father, into Your hands I commend My spirit" (Luke 23:46).

My last sermon before my arrest was on the awesomeness of God. My congregation did not understand much of it. Neither did I, and I wondered about what I said. Now I begin to understand, because I understand less and less about what God is doing with me.

How beautiful is the bride of Christ when she does not try to understand the Unintelligible, but follows Him blindly, and embraces Him in love. Amen.

CHAPTER 10

Exoteric Religion

DEAR BROTHERS AND SISTERS,

"The first living creature was like a lion, the second living creature like a calf, the third living creature had a face like a man, and the fourth living creature was like a flying eagle" (Revelation 4:7).

The Christian pastor today needs many qualities. He must be a theologian of high degree; he must be a clever strategist with the skill to win battles; he must possess a practical organizing capacity; and he must be a revolutionary, preparing the way for the twenty-first century to be an age of Christ's dominion.

There are two sides to religion. There is ezoteric religion, a name which comes from the Greek word *ezos*, inner. In this religion you are taught the deep mysteries of God which are reserved for the few who truly seek them.

Then there is the exoteric side, from the Greek *exos*, outer, which is the practical day-to-day religion of the great majority of men.

The Book of Esther in the Bible is the prototype of exoteric religion, a religion which stops at the outward man and is concerned with national destinies. That is why this book never mentions the name of God. But a book of sheer politics forms part of the Holy Scripture, and has its honored place there, on an equal footing with the Song of Songs, a book of pure poetry.

Exoteric and ezoteric religion must go together.

We recently learned, from a new prisoner tapping on the wall in Morse code, that Tibet has been invaded by the Chinese Communists. The Tibetans had a purely mystical religion, which did not equip them for diplomacy and political fighting. Now politics will entirely wipe out the mysticism. That is the fate of mysticism, if it is not allied with right political thought.

Those who are prepared to understand the mysteries of the kingdom of God are few. Let the other Christians be drawn into political activity which will serve to the glory of the same kingdom. Then the spiritually wise, like the apostles of old, will be able to withdraw from serving at tables and devote themselves to the spiritual world. They will live only in the realm of truth, undistracted by material problems, an involvement which can bring harm both to them and to the material world.

The fall of Adam was a premature initiation into mysteries. The deep designs of God cannot be plucked from a tree. A man must first learn over a long period to put aside selfish interests, and the interests of his social group, pride, passion and the judgment of other people's passions, prejudices, his sin and his righteousness. Only a holy man can know the whole truth accessible to mankind.

A man is prepared for the highest initiation, only if he can die on a cross with the words, "Father, forgive them, for they do not know what they do" (Luke 23:34).

All others have to remain in the lower spheres, in the realm of the exoteric. But how unspeakably useful they can be there! If there had been no Esther, the Jewish nation would have disappeared, there would have been no Jesus and no Christian civilization, and the gates of heaven would have been closed for many.

The Esthers, those who do not have the word "God" much on their lips, but who fight to keep the world free for the gospel, to liberate it from the dominion of communism and from heathen terror, are especially important today.

A group of people were once amusing themselves by considering which book they would choose to have with them on a desert island. A clergyman chose the Bible. Another man decided on the plays of Shakespeare. Another settled for a book of jokes to keep him amused. Then a wise man spoke, "I would choose a book which would teach me how to build a boat in which I could escape to the mainland. Once there, I would be able to decide what to read, whether it is the Bible, fine literature, or humor. But first of all I must be free."

Men must be free. Jesus teaches that only the truth can set us free. The converse is also true. Only freedom gives us truth. Under a dictatorship, truth is inaccessible. Fighters for freedom are fighters for truth, and therefore for God. The warriors of Cyrus, who were not worshipers of Yahweh, are called a holy army, because they freed from Babylonian captivity the Jews who were the repositories of the truth.

In Luke 6:1 there is a strange Greek word, what is called a *hapax*, a word that occurs only once in the Bible. In most translations it is rendered as "the second Sabbath after the first," which makes no sense. The word is *deuteroprotos*, literally translated "the second first." The translators did not know what to do with this word. Even Jerome considered it disrespectfully to be sheer nonsense. But it has a deep meaning.

A man must first seek the kingdom of heaven and its righteousness, and then care for his belly. But there are moments when the second things come first, moments of *deuteroprotos*. If on a Sabbath day you are so hungry that you have to pluck ears of corn and eat them, or if you have a hungry family to care for, second things come first. You must be concerned first for food and then for the sanctification of the Sabbath.

That is what the gospel teaches in Luke chapter 6. There are many things in life which are decidedly of secondary importance, but which can put you at a given moment under such high pressure that you have to treat them as priorities.

That is how it is with liberty.

Forget about deep theological musings, for which most of you are not intended (those who are made for it will ignore my appeal to forget it) and instead become political fighters against the Communist oppression. It was something like this that Joan of Arc did, and she came to be recognized as a religious heroine.

Is there any hope that your fight will succeed? Reason tells you no. Bolshevism has reigned for decades undisturbed in Russia. Now it has conquered half of Europe and infiltrated the other half.

Reason tells you that yours is a vain fight, just as reason told David that he could not overcome Goliath. It is a characteristic of the Christian that he accepts things which seem absurd to reason. Reason, by believing that the earth revolves round the sun, believes what is absurd to the senses. Why should we not treat reason as it treats the senses? Why should we not transcend reason?

Jesus teaches that only the truth can set us free. The converse is also true. Only freedom gives us truth.

The human mind has gone mad, and you attain reality only when you pass beyond reason.

"The Son of Man is coming at an hour when you do not expect Him" (Matthew 24:44). When any thought of victory is abandoned, He will come and make you triumph. Don't be concerned about your chances of immediate success, but continue to fight for freedom.

There is another kind of knowledge than that given by reason. Love has a greater knowledge than logic. The Hebrew word *iada*, to know, and the Greek word *gnosis*, knowledge, are both related to sexual union, as in "Adam knew [*iada*] Eve" (Genesis 4:1). The man who unites himself in burning love with the world which suffers under slavery knows more than the strategists and the politicians. He knows that the God who did not allow the Jews to be slaves of the Egyptians has remained the same God who hates the slavery imposed today by Communists upon hundreds of millions of Chinese, Vietnamese, Laotians, and others. He hates any slavery and social injustice.

In the preamble to the Ten Commandments, God does not

say, "I am the Lord your God, who created heaven and earth," but, "I am the Lord your God, who brought you out of the land of Egypt, out of the house of bondage" (Exodus 20:2). To free slaves is a bigger honor for Him than to be the Creator of the universe.

Rely on Him, and fight. Fight on the level of earthly needs. "I have told you earthly things," says Jesus (John 3:12). I, too, have told you earthly things today. Fight to overthrow communism. If you are hearing me from even more distant places, fight to overthrow heathen terror, racial hatred, and all the godless rulers.

CHAPTER 11

Problems of an Underground Church

DEAR BROTHERS AND SISTERS,

Perhaps some of you have met the fighters of the underground church of the Soviet Union when the Red Army invaded our country. What beautiful characters they were, but what intriguing and gruesome stories they told us about their lives.

Now the best of you who are outside prison have no alternative: you must organize an underground work. The official churches either will be closed, or will accept Communist limitations on how much of the gospel can be proclaimed. The small legal opportunities that the Communists leave must be used to the maximum. But we will accept their fragments of freedom on the point of a spear. We will fight to be able to proclaim the whole, which will be possible only in a church like that which existed in the catacombs of Rome. Except that the conditions of modern life, the perfection of police methods and equipment, will make the task much harder.

It makes sense to attempt only what you are able to perform. The Christians of the Soviet Union could organize an underground church. So we shall succeed, too. But I do not approve of everything our Russian brethren told us. Their stories of the heroism of the martyrs thrilled and inspired us. But the best underground church is surely that which has the least number of martyrs, just as the best spy ring is one that remains forever undiscovered. It is not martyrs we want, but victories.

Be careful about accepting new members into the underground church. To be a member of an ordinary church, you have to fulfill two obligations: to believe and to be baptized. Some denominations consider you a member even if you don't believe, once you have been baptized. But acceptance into the underground church lets a man in on secrets. He will know hidden meeting places and pastors who are wanted by the police. If he cracks under torture, he may destroy a whole organization. To be baptized and to believe is not enough. Paul was a convert for only three days, but he had to be told about one further condition: "how many things he must suffer for My name's sake" (Acts 9:16).

The capacity to suffer is an absolutely necessary condition for being a member of the underground church. You must teach converts from the very beginning to be like Paul, who submitted to whippings, beatings, countless perils, and imprisonment for the sake of the gospel. They will have to bear such pain with patience, with joy, and with thankfulness.

But it is not only torture for which they must be prepared. Beatings and a certain amount of torture can be borne by every well-prepared Christian who is filled with the Holy Spirit. But just as the atomic weapon is absolute and irresistible, so there are some tortures that men cannot stand. Under torture, Savonarola recanted, and Cranmer's courage deserted him and he repudiated his own writings. Under such torture Thomas Munzer recanted, too, and so did many Catholic heroes tortured by the Protestants. Here in prison, sometimes the most refined cruelties are committed. In the limited sphere in which our Morse-code system operates, I know only one or two who did not confess when submitted to such pressure. Neither do I know what would have happened if it had been continued with me. But happily, these heavy tortures are very rare, because the torturers themselves cannot bear them. Man is not made to inflict agony upon his fellow men. Even torturers may have religious mothers, wives, or children, who chide them for what they do. There is no perfect criminal, nor is there a perfect torturer. He tires of his job.

The Russian Christians told us that in the Soviet Union the Communists have succeeded after thirty years in creating a new type of being, the "anti-man," a man who can over years inflict extreme torture and not flinch. The Nazis also created such a species. In Romania we have not yet gone so far.

But still, you must be prepared for the worst. The newest convert must be told that not only may he have to pass through terrible physical pain, but he may also become a traitor after having suffered much for Christ. We need not frighten him unduly, but neither can we deceive him. He must know all the risks in which he will be involved.

> The convert must know he may starve to death in prison. God must simply be served.

The convert will have to give up all romantic expectations. He must know that a foolhardy enterprise, a superhuman task, awaits him.

It is said that Hudson Taylor, founder of the China Inland Mission, when told to form a committee so he would have the necessities of life in a country so far away, replied, "I have no difficulty in remembering that my children need breakfast and dinner. Is it possible to imagine that our heavenly Father is less tender and mindful of His children than I?" A beautiful sentiment, but romantic. I have had no breakfast for two years. Dinners I have had. I wonder if Hudson Taylor would have called them dinners. The convert must know that he has no guarantee from God that he will have breakfasts or lunches. He must know that he may starve to death in prison, without any hand stretching out from heaven to feed him. God must simply be served. If or what He will give you in return for this is incalculable.

Some believers in Communist nations have committed suicide rather than risk betraying their brothers and sisters. We must let God decide the morality of their decision.

To protect the church from the Secret Police, you will have to infiltrate the latter. This you can do only by deceiving, concealing, accepting the necessity for lying. This ought not to be a moral problem. Christians who are undercover agents in democratic countries do the same when they infiltrate criminal circles and spy rings in order to serve their country and the cause of order. Why should it not be done for the good of the underground church?

There is a legend that when Herod had given the order to kill the children in Bethlehem, Mary and Joseph tried to escape with the Child. But the sentries at the gate stopped them. They asked Mary, "What are you carrying in your arms?" She answered, "A bunch of lilies." "Unwrap your bundle and show us." She unwrapped it with confidence. They saw only lilies, and allowed her to pass. Was Mary lying? Did God strengthen a lie with a miracle? Or did God change the Child at that moment into a bunch of lilies, as Catholics believe that bread and wine are changed into His body and blood during the communion service? Did Mary hope that God would make the soldiers have an optical illusion? Some may wonder that I ask serious questions in connection with a legend. But you know me. You know that for me the world of legend and myth is reality.

The Creator shows us the whole creation other than as it is. It took men thousands of years to discover that the earth revolves around the sun, and that our entire world is a whirlwind of elementary particles. God does not seem keen to tell us the whole truth. Why should I tell it to a Communist officer? We have to discover God's realities; let the Communists work to try to discover our organization. It is not my business to tell him the facts about it.

The Russian underground church, as it was described to us by its members and leaders, is not sufficiently sophisticated. They have not thought out these questions. That is why they have lost so many victims. A "sincere" underground pastor is no more possible than dry water or wooden iron.

They did not use codes in their exchange of letters. Some did, but the codes were primitive and ridiculously easy to decode.

Many other problems arise. Either we must renounce the idea of a well-organized underground church, in which case we will only furnish more and more victims to the Secret Police; or we must agree to use nicknames and false documents, to hide and distort facts. But this is exhausting for a man who is of the truth and yearns for it. Communists have worked secretly very successfully, but with them the lie is their very element. Christians will easily tire and, once they have compromised in their duty to always tell the truth, the door will be open for another compromise: why not come to an arrangement with the Secret Police and play a double role? We need men of steel. But with the amount of spiritual energy a man possesses at a certain moment being limited, we have to ban energy-robbing ideological controversies in order to concentrate the energy for the moments of great temptations and trials.

We must learn to discover the Communist spies within our ranks. Sometimes it will be quite easy. Just tell a suspected informer about an important meeting with top leaders at a certain address. This meeting must not on any account take place. But the address must be chosen so that you can observe the house secretly and see if there is police surveillance. You can apologize afterward to the informer for having given him wrong directions. If you have discovered an informer, keep him in the church. A known informer is good capital. By following him, you can discover the officers of the Secret Police with whom he is in touch and through these other informers. Don't give him his punishment too early.

A well-organized underground church needs money. It must have secret printing presses and secret broadcasting stations, the latter frequently changing their location because they can be traced. There will also be bribes to ensure warning of impending arrests, and other expenses. The Communists, when they were a secret organization, used to rob to help the Party. Stalin went to prison for committing such a robbery. They also forged money. Will our brethren from abroad give us material help? I hope so. They do not help the Russian underground church.

There was a Lazarite Catholic nun who tended a sick, lonely old man. His house was full of gold and silver objects that were of no practical use. She took first one thing then another, sold them and gave the money to the poor, keeping a strict account of what she did with it. When she was arrested, a French jury acquitted her. Did her conscience also acquit her? Napoleon said that to win a war you need money, money, and more money. I believe that this holds true for the war of the underground church as well, though money alone will not achieve it.

There will be many problems. As in the church in general, women will play an increasingly large role in the underground church. Some of the leaders will have to meet Christian women. They will often have to be alone together, probably late at night, without any witnesses. This will not happen only once or twice; it will be a general practice. Temptations will arise, which will be the more intense because underground workers will inevitably be under constant emotional and nervous strain, which tends to bring about an increase in sexuality. We learned about this from our Russian brethren. Paul wrote to an underground church in Corinth, "It is actually reported that there is sexual immorality among you" (1 Corinthians 5:1). Though this sin is common, he proposes expelling from the church only one, who had committed incest. Paul knew the difficulties of leading a pure sexual life in underground conditions, yet he commanded them to lead pure lives and not associate with believers who were sexually immoral.

> Every member must obey his conscience and his pastor, more than the state authorities.

Wives whose husbands have been in prison for years will have to meet with new underground pastors. There are certain temptations that must be faced and overcome.

As underground workers have to move about from place to place, meeting privately with women, unavoidable jealousies will arise. Jealousy may lead to denunciations, so great caution is needed. James, writing to underground churches, calls their members several times "my brethren" and then suddenly rebukes them as "adulterers and adulteresses" (James 4:4).

Every member must obey his conscience and his pastor, more than the state authorities. The pastor will have to be obeyed as strictly as in the army. There is no time, no place, for argument.

I am far from you, alone in a cell. May God give you wisdom to organize a powerful, well-trained underground church. Amen.

CHAPTER 12

You'll Be on the Right Side

D<small>EARLY BELOVED BROTHERS AND SISTERS</small>,

Today something seemingly impossible happened. The officer on duty came into my cell with a pot of honey in his hand. "This is from your brother Herescu; he brought it," he said. "A daring guy." Then he went out, locking the door behind him.

I have no bread, no spoon. I shall manage somehow. But Herescu has risked his liberty by bringing me a gift.

He will be on the right-hand side of Jesus on the day of judgment. I was in prison, and he visited me. Also on His right-hand side there will be the guard who sometimes passes a word from me to my family and back. So will be my wife, with two sisters.

Before I was put in this underground cell, I had a cell with a window facing the front entrance of the prison. One day, in a fit of depression, I asked God, "Where are You? Have You forsaken me?" At that very moment, I saw coming into the yard my wife, and Bianca and Alice, who had come to inquire about me. Since then, whenever I say "Lord," I see these three. When I think about these three, I see the Lord. I identify Christ with His believers.

All these will be at Christ's right side.

But what about the others who did not dare, those who did not even wish to move a finger in our defense, the millions of Christians who care nothing for the sufferings of their fellow believers? What will be their fate?

We pass about two-thirds of our life awake and another third in sleep, dreaming. What makes us believe that God will judge men only according to what they do while they are awake? If the whole life is examined, should not the dreams count also?

When I fall asleep, I see myself surrounded by so much love. People whom I knew to be the most selfish or apathetic, sometimes even my torturers, are bending over me tenderly, giving me food and drink, offering me flowers. All these people have visited me in prison, though they did it in my dreams. Does this count for nothing? If what happens in a dream is nothing, why is there a dream recorded on the very first page of the New Testament?

And surely it is not in my dreams only that they are good. Bad men are often very good in their own dream life. For many years I have paid close attention to what I see in my sleep, because I believe the Talmud is right when it says that a dream which is not understood is like a letter which has not been opened. I cannot agree with Freud that only our base and ugly impulses are expressed in dreams. If this were true, we should have to throw away the Bible, because it teaches just the opposite.

I have known Orthodox Jews who hated the very name of Jesus, which reminded them of anti-semitic Christians, but who dreamed of Him and were happy about it. Joseph, in the Old Testament, saw himself in his dreams as a ruler. But this did not express ambition. What happened later showed that what he meant by a ruler was a benefactor. In his dream God had shown him His great benevolent plans which embraced Joseph's whole family and whole countries, things which were not in his mind when he was awake.

The benzene ring was discovered in a dream. So the scientist who discovered it was wiser in his sleep than during the day, when he had sought in vain for the chemical formula.

Now, if a bad man dreams that he visits prisoners, feeds, washes and comforts them, should this have no validity before God? Which is which? A Chinese poet says, "I dreamed last night that I was a butterfly, and I do not know now whether I am a man who dreamed he was a butterfly, or a butterfly who dreams that he is a man." Why should we call someone a bad man rather than a likeable dreamer? Many great artists have led morally wretched lives. What of Oscar Wilde, Guy de Maupassant, Richard Wagner? We judge them according to their books and their music, which were so remote from their manner of life. Does God judge men according to their beautiful dreams rather than by their neglect of us when they are awake?

The Bible tells us that the angel of the Lord appeared to Joseph in a dream (Matthew 1:20). Do angels also dream? Do angels sleep? Is there a telepathic communication between sleeping beings? (You will forgive me. I am not entirely normal. Don't expect me to give normal sermons.)

> If God is the maker of all things, "visible and invisible," is He not the maker of the subconscious, too?

And how about the believers who have passed into the life beyond? Are they awake in paradise, or is their whole eternal life a continuous beautiful dream? Jesus said, "Our friend Lazarus sleeps" (John 11:11). Every other Jew would have said, "He is walking and worshiping now in God's paradise." Jesus also said that Jairus's daughter was sleeping.

I know myself, that in this cell my heaven is to fall asleep. At once the gray walls and the brutality disappear. Everything becomes beautiful, and even the wardens appear angelic.

At His judgment, God will keep in view the good which we do in dreams. "Christ died for us, that whether we wake or sleep, we should live together with Him" (1 Thessalonians 5:10). I thank you all who visit us in our prison cells while you sleep. You also will hear the words, "Come, you blessed of My Father, inherit the kingdom prepared for you from the foundation of the world" (Matthew 25:34).

The Coptic church honors Pontius Pilate as a saint, which seems very curious to those of us who do not allow God to forget his crime, reminding him of it as often as we recite the creed. (I wonder why this man alone has been singled out for condemnation.) There must have been something holy in Pilate. He did very wrong things. He gave Jesus to be scourged and crucified. But he also said some very good things: "I find no fault in this Man" (Luke 23:4). I understand criminals, because I myself have a criminal element in my nature and have committed the gravest offenses. Criminals often dream of themselves doing the most wonderful things. Pilate's remorse may have made him dream that he was caressing Jesus. The Coptic church may have judged him according to this.

When a Jew or a heathen says "No" to Jesus, do not look only at his conscious attitude. If God is the maker of all things, "visible and invisible," is He not the maker of the subconscious, too? Out of my subconscious there emerged one day the image of Jesus, and I loved it. But it had been there for a long time. Paul killed Christians. That is what men knew. But there was another side to him, of which he himself was unconscious, that he had been "separated from his mother's womb" to serve Christ (Galatians 1:15). Deep in his subconscious, there was the call. And one day the subconscious became conscious. It pleased God to reveal His Son in him. The wicked Saul or the saint Paul—it depends on how we look at him, whether we judge by superficial impressions or employ in-depth psychology.

What a crazy sermon! I would never have delivered it from a pulpit. But just take it as a dream of mine, that even torturers can have something good in them, at least when they are asleep. Dreams are madness, and that is why I am preaching today as I do. I should like to see our executioners saved.

And remember that the Old Testament praises Joseph, not as a man who lived intensely in his real life, but as a dreamer of dreams.

To look on a woman to lust after her pollutes me even if I have not touched her. Then what if I look on a woman with the thought of doing her good, even if I do nothing afterward? Righteousness demands that this also should be enough. Where is the miserable man who has never had any good in his intentions, in his looks, in his dreams?

Leave me with my foolish thoughts. I will still hope for you who have abandoned us, who have not visited us in prison in your waking hours. You too will be on the right side. Amen.

CHAPTER 13

The True Christian Teacher

DEAR BROTHERS AND SISTERS,

I can admit of no free lances in Christianity—Christians are soldiers who belong to an army. They have commanders, and must obey them. Christ Himself "gave some to be apostles...some pastors and teachers" (Ephesians 4:11). No one can be a Christian and declare Jesus as his only pastor, just as no one can obey a general while refusing obedience to the captain or even the sergeant, though these are much less competent than the commander-in-chief.

We used to live under a free enterprise system, and we have applied to our churches principles and ideas taken from this system. But Christianity is not of this world. There is no such thing as free enterprise in Christianity. There is organization, hierarchy, and, I repeat, obedience. Obedience not only toward God, but toward your fellow Christians "who rule over you" (Hebrews 13:7).

You have the right to ask, "Well, then, who is the pastor in whom I should have confidence?" It is his task to bring me to maturity as a saint, but there are so many fakes. Some men who are called pastors don't even have the intention of making men into saints. Those who believe they have this calling say so many contradictory things, and give so many contradictory examples of living that I am confused. Who is the true pastor?

This is a problem which is not yours alone. Christ has it, too. He asks, "Who then is a faithful and wise servant, whom his master made ruler over his household, to give them food in due season?" (Matthew 24:45) and he finishes the thought with a question mark. So much He knew; so much He said. He could give you no clear indication of where to find the right pastor. He could not tell you to rely on the Bible alone. The Bible teaches you about faithful servants who will give you the Word of God. To give men the Bible alone as a sufficient rule is like giving the pupils in a school all the books, without guiding their reading. They need more than books. They need a teacher.

But what has Christ revealed on the subject of who is the right teacher? His revelation was a question mark—one of many in the Bible. Who is the true bride of Christ? Would you like to know? Look it up in the Scriptures, and you will find God's answer in the Song of Solomon 3:6. There is posed the same question that you are asking, "Who is she [so says the original] that comes out of the wilderness like pillars of smoke, perfumed with myrrh and frankincense, with all powders of the merchant?" Look carefully at the answer which follows. It is a question mark. Just that. Question marks are God's only revelations concerning some of the biggest problems of the Christian life, such as how to find the right pastor, and how to be sure which is Christ's true bride. In the original, even the question mark is missing. There is just a blank space, a stimulus to thought.

God wants us to find the answers for ourselves. We are in the paradoxical position that we have to be taught matters of faith by God-approved teachers, but we must know these matters beforehand so well that we are able ourselves to choose the right teacher from among hundreds who offer themselves as guides. It is a paradox, like all the paradoxes of life. In order to extract iron, you need iron tools. In order to have iron tools, you must extract iron from the mines, which you cannot do without having the tools first. Theoretically, the extraction of iron is an impossibility. But life has shown itself stronger than theory.

You have the same thing here. You begin with very primitive

tools, in this case with very simple criteria. With these you can make the first steps toward discovering the right teacher. Having found him, you will progress further, together with him—since he also is only a man—but guided by him.

One very primitive criterion for discovering the right teacher is to ask, "How long has he kept silent?"

The soul does not leave a place at the same speed as the body. A messenger from God cannot deliver his message at once. His spirit continues for a long time to dwell in the heavenly places where he received the message.

When I was arrested, it was a long time before my spirit came to stay with me in prison. To begin with, it remained at home. It took the Holy Spirit thirty years to reach Jesus. Empowered by the descending of the Spirit, He could then deliver His message. John the Baptist also had to wait thirty years.

Paul, after having seen and heard Jesus, and after having received instruction in the proper manner from a pastor, Ananias, went to Arabia to meditate in loneliness. He was not good yet as a messenger. His soul was still tossed to and fro by tempests, and continued to dwell for a long time in the old Pharisaic framework. Only after many years did his soul realize what his ears and eyes had perceived. After this he became fit to be an apostle.

Slowness to speak is generally a characteristic of a Christian (James 1:19)—even more so of the righteous teacher. A man who has not passed years in silent meditation may be able to give you a useful interpretation of messages delivered by others in times gone by, but he is not a reliable teacher. Why should you receive messages second hand and not directly from the source?

How long has the would-be teacher been silent? Ask him this question: "How long have you been non-existent, of no standing at all in the spiritual life?" This is the only guarantee against pride. The man who does not stand on a height can never fall.

A second characteristic of the true teacher is that he will use language of a different quality. The officers who went to arrest Jesus returned saying, "Never man ever spoke like this Man!" (John 7:46). Unquestionably, many of the teachings of Jesus existed also in the Old Testament, in the Jewish tradition, in the Vedas, in Meng-Tse and Lao-Tse. They were similar to the teachings of Rabbi Hillel. Jesus used words common to religion and mysticism in all times. Otherwise nobody would have understood Him. But, along with all this, there was a uniqueness in the language He spoke which startled men as they had been startled —to a lesser degree—whenever they had met a prophet before. What the true teacher of God has to say cannot be described in terms of common concepts, because God's thoughts are not like our thoughts. Our languages and concepts have been formed since time began to enable communication between men in hunting, fishing, producing food, and in personal relationships. From where could we have found the words to convey a divine message?

> Pastors have to be makers of saints and not of logically well-connected systems.

The true messenger from God cannot find adequate words in any human language. Neither can he fit his message into the much-too-simple patterns of logic. So many words are homonyms, and when I use a word in one sense, a secondary meaning passes simultaneously through my mind, creating thought associations that have nothing to do with logic. Words alone, and their logical connections, are quite unfit to express a divine message. Logically well-constructed, systematic theologies, and highly logical sermons come rather from the devil.

Goethe knew the devil, and in *Faust* he puts into the mouth of Mephistopheles these words to a young student:

Waste not your time, so fast it flies.
Method will teach you time to win.
Hence, my young friend, I would advise,
With college logic to begin.

Then will your mind be so well braced,
In Spanish boots so tightly laced,
That on 'twill circumspectly creep,
Thoughts beaten track securely keep.

Nor will it, *ignis-fatuus* like,
Into the path of error strike.
Then many a day they'll teach you how
The mind's spontaneous acts, till now

As eating and as drinking free,
Require a process—one, two, three.
In truth the subtle web of thought
Is like the weaver's fabric wrought.

One treadle moves a thousand lines,
Swift dart the shuttles to and fro,
Unseen the threads unnumber'd flow,
A thousand knots one stroke combines.

Then forward steps your sage to show,
And prove to you it must be so.
The first being so and so the second,
The third and fourth deduc'd we see.

And if there were no first and second,
Nor third nor fourth would ever be.
This, scholars of all countries prize,
Yet 'mong themselves no weavers rise.

Who would describe and study aught alive,
Seeks first the living spirit thence to drive.
Then are the lifeless fragments in his hand,
There only fails, alas—the spirit-band.

Logic is a subtle web of thoughts, but they are only thoughts, and so they remain. Pastors have to be, according to Ephesians 4:11,12, makers of saints and not of logically well-connected systems.

Ordinary language is not enough for the true messenger of God. That is why David and Deborah used song, accompanying the words with music. That is why the first Christians used to dance, according to gnostic sources. That is why the church has always expressed its message in sculpture and painting and ceremonial.

And even these are not enough. Consider how much Jesus spoke without words. The Gospels continually remark that "He lifted his eyes," "He lifted his hand," "He touched." He spoke not with words only, but with gestures, with the expression of His face. Look at Rubens' picture of the driving out of the merchants, and you will have some idea of how much the face of Jesus must have spoken.

In a true message from God, the significant silences play also an exceptional role.

Many assert their belief in the Bible as the Word of God. But if you examine them more closely, you will find out that they do not really believe it. The Bible consists of white sheets of paper (in the early days, of parchment), with black letters inscribed on them. Nearly all Christians believe the black letters to be God's Word. But the white pages do not have a place in their creed. Yet these are of enormous importance.

Luke says that at the age of twelve, Jesus was in the temple and all the teachers were astonished at His answers (Luke 2:46,47). You will seek for these answers in vain in the black letters of the Bible. They are on the white pages.

Mary chose "the good part." She sat at the feet of Jesus and heard His words (Luke 10:38–42). This may be interesting, but I would rather like to know what was the word to which she listened. This is reported in the Bible, but not in the black letters. You must learn to read the white pages. There you will also find the solution to the mystery of what Jesus did between the ages of twelve and thirty.

The Bible is a message from God, and speaks through its silences, not only through its words. Music is beautiful not only in its notes, but also in its pauses.

Try to understand the silences of God's messengers. The truer the messenger, the more mysterious his silences. He often speaks a great many words to cover the silence about the deepest things. You have to go beyond his words to find the truth which he means to convey.

Discover the mystery beyond the words of the messenger, and you will know the message from God.

But what if you cannot find a teacher with the characteristics

I have described? Then you yourself may be a righteous teacher in the process of formation. You can put these things to your pastor, and in this way you can be very helpful to him. The relationship between the pastor and his parishioner is a paradox. The parishioner learns from the pastor. But it is also true that he has to form him.

In everything you do, begin by accepting these criteria.

I am sorry that I was never a good Christian teacher. I had not yet had my time in Arabia. Now I live in complete silence, absolutely alone. The guards have felt-soled shoes. I don't hear their approach. They give me my food without saying a word. Inner voices have also ceased. For long periods not even God speaks to me. My conscience keeps quiet, too.

Perhaps God is reforming me to be a good teacher in the future. Pray for this. Amen.

CHAPTER 14

Salt Is Good

DEAR BROTHERS AND SISTERS,

When Jews get up in the morning, they first wash themselves, and then immediately start their prayers, which last for at least an hour. Christians, on the other hand, first read the Bible and only afterward begin to pray.

Why?

The Rabbi David Talner, contrary to the normal custom of the Jews, used to start the day by reading his mail, and only prayed afterward. When asked why, he answered, "The more renowned a man is, the more difficult is his struggle against besetting evil thoughts in prayer. So I always read my letters first. Usually, they begin by addressing me as a righteous rabbi, a teacher, a leader, a holy man, or by some other complimentary phrase. Then I begin my prayer saying, 'Lord, you know that I do not deserve these titles of honor. But since so many men believe me to be so in all sincerity, do not put their faith to shame. Make me become what they believe I am.'"

This is the reason we read the Bible before praying. Through the Bible, not men, God Himself speaks to us the most beautiful and undeserved words, "You are the salt of the earth" (Matthew 5:13). "You are the light of the world" (Matthew 5:14). "You are all sons of God" (Galatians 3:26), "partakers of the divine nature" (2 Peter 1:4), "heirs of God" (Romans 8:17). "I have loved you with an everlasting love" (Jeremiah 31:3). This incites us to prayer that we may become what we are called by God.

But as in Shakespeare's *The Tempest*, Antonio, a usurper, "made such a sinner of his memory to credit his own lie—he did believe he was indeed the duke," so it is easy for us to take as realities compliments which spring from love and are a call to goodness. We can easily believe a lie; we can believe that we are indeed what we are deemed to be, without any striving to attain the qualities of these titles.

We are the salt of the earth. Jesus says, "Salt is good" (Mark 9:50). I wonder what made Him say those simple words. Did He ever eat unsalted food? One time our guards poured spoonfuls of salt down our throats, and then left us without water. Now, on the contrary, we have for months been given completely unsalted food. For us, these oats boiled in water, without any salt, are absolutely unbearable. We sometimes prefer to go hungry and do not eat them. Primitive peoples, once they taste salt brought by traders, long for it. Travelers in some parts of Africa are surrounded by men begging for a little salt. We who are deprived of it know that "salt is good." The idea that Jesus spent part of His youth in countries far from Palestine, perhaps in countries where salt was not known, might not be entirely invention.

Now, if "you are the salt of the earth," and "salt is good," are we good? Are we seasoning the meals of other men? Are we giving taste and sense to other men's lives? Or do we leave them without salt, as we prisoners are left? The simple fact that the Bible calls us salt is not enough. A friend of mine, a teacher, had a pupil who had great possibilities but was lazy. Once he handed in a bad thesis. The teacher reproached him for this, but gave him the highest mark, telling him, "Now you have got this mark, try to deserve it in the future."

But how do we become good? The conditions do not seem to be very favorable. At first, I did not exist. Then I was made, from the very same elements from which the dust of the earth is formed. Soon, I shall be dust again. My soul has inherited a sinful character. There is no possibility of my becoming good by any act of my will. Neither can my will keep me good. We have to rely utterly on the grace of God. You have become good when you have made the great discovery that you are not good, and cannot be so. Then you ask God to make you so. The result is that you die, and you become another person—you become He. All His righteousness becomes yours, not a particle less than it was His. You are as much entitled to proclaim yourself the owner of His righteousness and goodness as you are to proclaim yourself the owner of any estate which has been given you legally as a gift, or which you have inherited. A Christian can say to Jesus, like St. Gertrude, "You are I!"; or like Luther in his commentary on the Epistle to the Galatians, "A Christian is Christ."

> You can as little lose your divine nature as Christ can cease to be Christ.

By putting on Christ's personality, by being clothed in Him, by being able to say, "It is no longer I who live, but Christ lives in me" (Galatians 2:20), you are the salt of the earth, you are good and will remain so forever. The question as to how the salt will be seasoned again if it has lost its saltiness becomes purely theoretical, because for you it can never happen that the salt should lose its saltiness; you can as little lose your divine nature as Christ can cease to be Christ.

Now, how should I proceed practically to be not me, but Him? The Bible speaks of the foolishness of the cross (1 Corinthians 1:18), and even about the foolishness of God (1 Corinthians 1:25). So, let us learn from the madmen.

There are madmen who believe that they are Napoleon. Others reckon themselves to be St. Francis of Assisi or Winston Churchill. Each behaves according to what he reckons himself to be. The man who thinks he is Napoleon will put on a tricorne hat, keep his right hand in the breast of his jacket, discuss military strategy, and boast about Austerlitz or curse the English for having defeated him at Waterloo. Those who think they are St. Francis will wear the habit and girdle of a monk, will fast and pray a great deal and speak holy phrases, even if they do not make sense. The man who reckons himself to be Churchill will always go about with a thick cigar in his mouth and talk about politics. What you reckon yourself to be determines your behavior.

Begin with this madness. Consider yourself what St. Gertrude and so many other believers have considered themselves to be: you are He. This mad presupposition will have the same result as with other madmen. More and more, you will come to behave like Him.

There is a difference, though, between the two kinds of madness. If you consider yourself to be Churchill, you behave like Churchill, but you are not Churchill. But if I believe myself to be He, an essential part of His mystical body (just as my heart is me, and my brain is me, and my glands and my soul and my spirit and my eyes; so every member of His body is He) and if this produces in me step by step the corresponding changes, then I am really He. The words of the Bible, "As He is, so are we in this world" (1 John 4:17), have found their fulfillment.

It needs faith to believe yourself to be He when you are a sinner. But what do we really know about the lives of the prophets, from Isaiah to Malachi? We know their prophecies, not their virtues and failures. You become a child of God by faith, not by virtues and good deeds.

Have this faith, and you will be essentially good, with a goodness that cannot fade away. The salt can never lose its saltiness. This or that bit of salt can lose it. Salt, the chemical formula; salt, the notion; salt in its essence, can never cease to be salt. You will become the unalterable formula of "goodness."

Cease your own life completely. Deny the self. Cease to practice its virtues as much as its lusts. You have been crucified with Christ, and have suffered the fate of every crucified man. You have died. But you exist. Since you exist after having died, you must have been born again, this time not from an earthly union; you have not been conceived in sin, but are begotten from God. You are once again a child. (According to the Talmud, the etymology of "cherub" is *kerabja*, like a child, because in Babylon a child was called *rabja*.) You have been born with a new, divine character. Believe it.

Don't be disturbed if you continue to see evil in yourself. Children see many fancies. Their world is populated with many products of their imagination. Rather believe the word of God: "In those days and in that time,...the iniquity of Israel shall be sought, but there shall be none; and the sins of Judah, but they shall not be found" (Jeremiah 50:20). This refers to the time of the return of the Jews from Babylonian captivity. Looked at from the human level, they had plenty of sins. Nehemiah punished some of them for this. From the godly level, which is now yours, they had none. Self-diagnosis is no good. Do not judge yourself. Only believe steadfastly that it is not you who live, but He. Continue to believe it, just as the madman believes himself to be Napoleon although everyone contradicts him, and you will succeed. You will achieve the goodness that does not fade. Amen.

CHAPTER 15

Believe in What Flows from Your Heart

DEAR BROTHERS AND SISTERS,

How, in practice, does God command a child of His what to speak? It happens in different ways. He can do it through a dream. I once dreamed an article for a magazine, from beginning to end. I was so shaken by the dream that I awoke and wrote it down in the middle of the night. The article has been spoken of as one of my best. It was also an accurate prediction of my future spiritual journeys, although I did not understand this at the time.

Another time I dreamed a whole sermon, beginning with "Beloved brethren" and finishing with "Amen." This too I wrote down during the night. (I never went to bed without having paper and pen near me. "I sleep, but my heart is awake," says the bride in the Song of Songs 5:2. She is continually waiting for some communication from the bridegroom.) This sermon seemed to me so fantastic that I never delivered it. Only after I had gone to prison did I realize that, if I had preached it, it would have warned my church of much suffering and could have halted some who were already sliding down the path of betrayal.

God does not speak only in dreams. Once at midday in the busiest part of Bucharest, I felt a compulsion to take out paper and pencil, and write down what would be given to me. I rested my paper against a shop window, and in half an hour the outline of a whole booklet was dictated to me. It became known as *The Mirror of the Human Soul,* and some consider it the best thing I have written. I don't shrink from repeating this tribute, because I had no part in writing the book.

I imagine that many children of God have experienced similar inspiration, either when awake or asleep.

At other times, God speaks through a verse of Scripture, a sermon, a book, or a conversation. But the most usual way in which He speaks to one of His children is, probably, by insinuating Himself into our own thought process. He commands me through my own character. I believe that my thoughts are His, even if these thoughts seem very odd to me. Many of the thoughts expressed in the psalms of David, or in the prophecies of Jeremiah or Ezekiel, and attributed to God, must have seemed very peculiar to the prophets.

Be yourself, speak what you think, and—if you are a child of God by faith—you can be sure that you have spoken what God has commanded you to speak. If not He, who else? He could change Balaam's curses into blessings, against the false prophet's will (Numbers 23,24). So He can change my words before I have uttered them. Since He does not do so, He must wish me to say the very words which I speak. Have your words sometimes been enticing words? Don't be afraid that because of this they were not words from God. The Lord sends enticing spirits (2 Chronicles 18:18–21). Perhaps He wants to destroy some Ahab who deserves it, and is using you as His instrument.

You would prefer to be used for other purposes? But society needs both perfumed ladies and evil-smelling tanners. Why should another man be the tanner, while you are the one who spreads intoxicating fragrances? Just put yourself at the disposal of God. Be His voice, as John the Baptist was, just a voice, allowing Him to be the mind that decides what the voice will say. John, the voice, spoke of Jesus having a fan in His hand and burning up the chaff with unquenchable fire (Matthew 3:12). The same divine mind later used the same voice to say that the one described so harshly was "the Lamb of God who takes away the sin of the world!" (John 1:29). John the Baptist was not concerned with how far the two utterances agreed. He simply said what flowed out of his mind, which he had yielded to God. You must do the same.

St. Bonaventure says that the devil proceeds against us like a general who sets out to capture a city. He finds out which is its weakest point, and there he attacks. Our weakest point is not to believe that God wills, speaks, and works through us.

It is written that "the king of Syria had commanded the captains of the chariots who were with him, saying 'Fight with no one small or great, but only with the king of Israel'" (2 Chronicles 18:30). This is the devil's strategy. Our most truly royal characteristic, the full assurance that we are entitled to behave and speak as we do, is the target for his attack.

> Our weakest point is not to believe that God wills, speaks, and works through us.

So the doubt arises in our mind, and in that of our hearers, whether we might have presumed to speak a word in God's name that God has not commanded us to speak. That is how the whole confusion arises.

Jesus knew Himself to be the truth. He knew that in everything He spoke, He said exactly what God meant Him to say, and in the way in which God intended. He had not the slightest doubt. How could anyone doubt who asserts, "I am the truth" (John 14:6)?

On the basis of this text, for nearly two thousand years the church has continued to assert that He is the truth. But He never proclaimed that He, Jesus, considered as a third person, is the truth. He said very clearly, "*I* am the truth"; I am this only as long as I am an I, a first person. A Jesus who is a he, a man who lived two thousand years ago in Palestine, cannot be the truth. He never expressed His opinions about such modern questions as the theory of relativity, modern technical or political life, the problems of Nazism, Bolshevism, and Imperialism, and so on.

Only a Jesus who is an I, a living I, can answer each day's problem.

Even in the most modest witness to the truth, He is an I. He lives through His witness with all the power of His truth, in the first person, giving to the disciple His own full confidence in everything he says and does. Some of the things the witness says may be erroneous from a human point of view. But God allowed those words. A chess player may sacrifice a pawn in order to win a game. The pawn may blame itself for the fact that it is captured. But it does not know what role this apparent loss may play in the strategic plan of the master.

God may have told Shimei to curse David (2 Samuel 16:5). He certainly willed that Caiaphas and Pilate should behave toward Jesus exactly as they did behave. The apostles said it, "Against Your holy servant Jesus, whom You anointed, both Herod and Pontius Pilate, with the Gentiles and the people of Israel, were gathered together to do whatever Your hand and Your purpose determined before to be done" (Acts 4:27,28). From a human point of view, they committed a crime in killing Jesus. From the divine viewpoint, they would have committed a crime by not crucifying Him, thus hindering the redemption of the world; this in the vain supposition that they had free will and could have done otherwise than they did.

I know that I am shocking you by talking like this. That is just what I want to do. Shocks can cure deafness. An enormous possibility is opened to you: to live free from doubts, free from the fear that you may do or say something contrary to the commandments of God; because Jesus, the truth, has become "I" in you by faith.

Do you believe that you have become the temple of the Holy Spirit? Then, being sure that the Holy Spirit is God, be also assured that He will allow nothing evil to dwell in this fair house of His.

John writes in his first epistle to the believers, "You have an anointing from the Holy One, and you know all things" (1 John 2:20). Jeremiah tells us the terms of the new covenant: "No more shall every man teach his neighbor, and every man his brother, saying, 'Know the Lord,' for they shall all know Me, from the least of them to the greatest of them, says the Lord" (Jeremiah 31:34). A Christian knows that what he knows is right. He need take no thought about what to speak. What flows out spontaneously from his new heart is God-given (Matthew 10:19).

But does he never make a mistake? Dr. Erlich made 665 unsuccessful experiments before he discovered the remedy for syphilis, a remedy therefore called 666. Were the first 665 unsuccessful experiments errors? You may call them that. You might just as well call them 665 steps upward toward the truth. Only in this sense does a Christian err. Every error of his is a necessary, unavoidable step toward the ultimate truth that lives within him, waiting only for the Christian to dig deeply enough within himself to find it. For him, to be a false prophet is no longer possible.

I have been through a terrible period of doubt. For weeks, the devil has tormented me every night, telling me that I have been a false prophet and am being punished for it. One night I made the decision to return to the Jewish faith. Another time I felt a strong compulsion toward the Church of Rome. But what if the Adventists were right? The Bible tells us hundreds of times to keep the Sabbath. To know that Jesus is the truth was of no help to me at that time. I recovered my serenity when I told the devil who tempted me, "I am the truth." Jesus, who is the truth, lives in me. That is the reality. Amen.

CHAPTER 16

Dull Genealogies

Beloved brothers and sisters,

Those passages in the Bible that appear to us to be boring genealogies or lists of places on a journey have in reality a deep significance.

Almost without exception, Hebrew names of towns and people have a specific meaning. It is therefore possible to read certain Bible verses in the original either as mere enumerations of names, or as sentences in which every word has a meaning. So, for example, commenting on Numbers 21:18–20, "And from the wilderness they went to Mattanah, from Mattanah to Nahaliel, from Nahaliel to Bamoth, and from Bamoth, in the valley," the Babylonian Talmud says, "If you become like the sand of the wilderness on which everyone can tread, you go to *matanah* (in Hebrew, gift), that is, you receive the gift of the Law. From there you go to *Nahali-El* (my inheritance is God). God becomes your inheritance. From here you go to *Bamoth* (this means to the heights). But if, once there, you become proud, you will descend again from the peaks into the valley." I remembered this part of the Talmud when they ordered me to lie down and then trod on me. That is the way to Mattanah.

Many Bible verses take on a new meaning when you know them in the original languages. At least pastors and priests should be required to know these. When people of different nationalities love each other, they usually learn one another's language. Why do children of God, especially those who are cultured, not learn the original language of the Bible? It made a great impression on me when I once read that, many years ago, a missionary visited the shop of a Chinese Christian at a time when he had no customers. He found him at his counter studying the New Testament in Greek. Amazed, he asked him how he had come to learn Greek. The shopkeeper answered, "Out of respect for the Word of God."

In the Book of Nehemiah there is a verse which has a deeper significance than appears on the surface, "Jeshua begot Joiakim, Joiakim begot Eliashib, Eliashib begot Joiada" (Nehemiah 12:10).

Jeshua is the first link in this genealogy. Jeshua is the name of the Savior in Hebrew; it is the equivalent of Jesus and means "salvation." We usually think of Jesus as saving us only from the punishment of our sins. We would like sin without hell, which is its unavoidable result. But He saves us from hell, as well as from sin, and from so much more. He saves us from error. God made Him to be for us not only ransom and redemption, but wisdom, too. He saves us from a life without meaning, without aim, and without vision. He saves us from pettiness.

For Ibsen's Peer Gynt, his self was "the host of desires, passions, and lust." It was the sum of caprice and all demands, in short "everything which belongs to me alone and is made to show my manner of being." He was sufficient to himself, forgetting that he came from someone else and depended on others for his life.

Jesus, Jeshua, saves us from this miniscule self. While Peer Gynt roamed for years about the world as a drunkard, a magician, a false prophet, a merchant of slaves, his real self lived on in the faith, hope, and love of Solveig, who waited for him faithfully.

Jesus gives us His self to be ours. What a delight it was, and is, for Him to have suffered for us, to share all our shortcomings, our failures, and our inability to rise above ourselves. He saves to the uttermost.

This Jeshua, salvation, begets in us Joiakim, which means "God raises us." Now we are fit to be raised to great heights. We are no more burdened by sins; we have been saved from attachment to transitory things.

This in turn begets Eliashib, "God turns to us." Glory be to God on high! It is not right that God should always descend to the level of our human misery. His plan is to raise us to the place where His throne is, to show us the beauties of His kingdom. Christ has dined with us. Now we shall enter into fellowship with Him, share in His divine thoughts, and help to fulfill His divine tasks.

Eliashib begets Joiada, which means "to know God." Before passing through all these stages, we may have known a good deal about God. Now we know Him. The Greek word for "knowledge," as well as the Hebrew, also contains the meaning of intimate union. "Adam knew Eve his wife" (Genesis 4:1). Now the time has come for the marriage of the Lamb. The wise virgins have entered with Him into the bridal chamber.

> This is the real aim of religion: to love God without restraint, and to never rest until you have been united with Him forever.

One state of heart begets another, one stage of spiritual growth begets another, just as a father begets a child. This is the deeper meaning of this verse, and of many other similar ones.

Rip off the mask and reveal the falsity which disguises itself as truth. Shun any religious guide who does not know this ancient way, trodden by the saints of old, and who does not walk in this path himself.

There are beauty shops for lies. You can dress them in priestly robes, surround them with the smoke of incense and with impressive organ music, and wrap them up in old or new theological assertions.

The truth is found somewhere else. It passes through the state of full salvation to that of being raised to high and heavenly places, where God turns to you in love and unites with you, embracing you with a holy kiss. This may happen in a splendid religious service, in a simple little chapel, at home, or in prison. But this is the real aim of religion: to love God without restraint, and to never rest until you have been united with Him forever.

The greater the pain, the more slowly the time passes. This is why God is eternal while we are transitory. He feels a pain so difficult to bear that we cannot even understand it. It is pain which causes His time never to pass.

In the Talmud it is written, "The night is divided into three watches. In every watch, the Holy One, blessed be His name, sits and roars like a lion, saying, 'Woe that I have destroyed My house. I have burned My temple and have banished My children among the nations... Woe to the father who has expelled his children, and woe to the children who have been driven out from the table of their father.'"

The pain of God must be made to cease, and this can only be done by rooting out its cause: our separation from Him. We must travel from Jeshua, through the intermediate stages, until we arrive at Joiada, in a union with God as complete as that of a bride with her husband. Then, with the pain of separation replaced by perfect happiness, time will fly quickly for God and for all those who know the joy of His presence. Time will pass so quickly that it will disappear completely. When this transition from salvation to union with God has occurred, God will be all in all. We shall sit with Him on His heavenly throne (Revelation 3:21). The aim of creation will have been fulfilled. The heirs of God will take over their inheritance.

We suffer remorse about all kinds of little sins. At the moment of the decisive crisis in our life, our greatest remorse will be not about our sins but about our religiosity, and our faith which has fallen short of this ultimate aim: to pass through full salvation, ascension, and His turning to us, into indissoluble union with Him.

St. Bonaventure said that a servant of God should examine himself seven times a day. Do we do this? And do we do it concerning what principally matters in religion—the mystical marriage with the Godhead?

This is depicted in communion. In it we unite with the Godhead in the person of Christ. We become one. He becomes flesh of our flesh and blood of our blood.

Before appearing before King Ahasuerus, the young maidens had to purify themselves for six months with oil of myrrh, and six months with perfumes (Esther 2:12). Even more so, we should purify ourselves and anoint ourselves with all that is best before uniting with Him in communion. Here again, Jeshua begets Joiakim, Joiakim begets Eliashib, and Eliashib begets Joiada. You become a temple for God. You can then rightly apply to yourself the words of David, "The work is great, because the temple is not for man but for the Lord God" (1 Chronicles 29:1).

David did not just begin building at random, but gathered a vast quantity of gold, silver, and jewels. The building passed through many stages until the glory of God came to dwell in it.

Your only true friend is the one who shows you this way, travels along it with you, and helps you as you go.

Which sense of ours shows us that a caterpillar is in the process of becoming a butterfly, or that an ugly egg is a future peacock? Our senses apprehend things statically, as they are at a given moment, not dynamically, as a process of change. So the sinners who confess to you are not only what your senses perceive.

A wicked man can be saved from his cruelty; a melancholic can be saved from his worries. Jesus can save everyone to the uttermost. Every soul can pass from Jeshua through Joiakim and Eliashib to Joiada, moving and living henceforth within the Godhead, indissolubly united with it.

When you see people in that way, it becomes progressively easier to overcome sensuality. Then the Spirit moves you, and you are able to overcome. Amen.

CHAPTER 17

God Is My Passion

MY DEAR CONGREGATION,

I wonder if a rich Christian farmer in the West, where farmers can still be rich, would be willing today to give for his religion the great quantity of bulls, lambs, rams, flour, oil, and wine, besides the obligatory tithes, which the Jews gave as offerings. The Israelites gave freely, and they gave out of poverty. Palestine may have been a blessed land, but the Jews of that time knew nothing of farming economy. They had nothing like the income of a modern Western farmer. But they gave so much that there came a time when Moses had to restrain them from giving any more, telling them, "Enough" (Exodus 36:3–7).

Religion for the Israelites was what it should be for every Christian: their ruling passion. A man who has a real passion, whether it be for gambling, drunkenness, womanizing, pride, or addiction to drugs, will give everything he has to satisfy it—his money, his honor, his health, his family. So it is with those who are passionately devoted to art, science, or politics. Fridtjof Nansen, passionate to know the secrets of the North Pole, lived there for three years among the polar bears. Men will die on the gallows for their revolutionary or reactionary ideals.

For your passion, you sacrifice everything. And religion is a passion. It calls for the sublimation of all evil lusts, and spending your human energies and possessions on God instead of on worldly things.

When you are young and have the fire in your blood, you do not keep account of how much your passion costs. So the Jews did not keep an exact account of their tithes. Besides the prescribed offerings, which were many, there were freewill offerings, some offered in fulfillment of vows made in difficult circumstances, some simply out of overflowing love to God. Religion is the state of heart of those who, more than anything else in the world, love, prize, and honor God.

A man cannot decide of his own free will whether or not to have a passion. No man is a drunkard or a chain-smoker because he decided to be one. He becomes one by a slow sliding into sin. You do not know at the beginning where it will lead you. The same thing happens with religion. It may begin by being just a legitimate curiosity that you experiment with as others might experiment with narcotics. From being an occasional practice, it can become a habit, and from this it develops into an irresistible passion.

Those in whom religion is not a passion for God are nevertheless not excluded from religion. They can be servants of those who have the passion. There are many people who work in breweries and tobacco factories, in the cinema industry, in printing shops which produce pornographic literature, or as smugglers of drugs, who, without having a passion themselves, help others to see their desires fulfilled. In a similar way, if you don't love God passionately, you can passionately love the passion for God which you don't possess; you can be a servant of the bride of Christ. Jesus said, "Whoever gives one of these little ones a cup of cold water in the name of a disciple…shall by no means lose his reward" (Matthew 10:42). Your reward will be that you will come to know the religious devotion for which you have longed. You will at last know passion for the Lord.

But this passion is shallow, so long as it is a passion for somebody else. At the beginning of *Romeo and Juliet*, Romeo is madly in love with Rosaline. It is enough for him to see another girl at a ball, to change his passion. Fortunately, both Romeo and Juliet die shortly afterward. Otherwise he might have changed the object of his love again. It is in the very nature of passions to be able to change their object. All the time you can see men passing from one ideal to another. Jesus said that you can only really love your neighbor if you love yourself. The highest measure of love for another is that which you have for yourself. The more you are aware of God's love for you, the more you will be able to love God. The more you are changed into Christ, the more Christ will become your passion, because He will be your real self.

Christians have almost forgotten the Orthodox teaching that they are being transformed into Christ even during this earthly life. St. Augustine recounts how he heard the voice of Christ saying, "I am the food of grown men; grow, and thou shalt feed upon Me; nor shalt thou convert Me, like the food of thy flesh, into thee, but thou shalt be converted into Me." St. Thomas Aquinas said that it is in the nature of the sacrament of communion to transform man into God, and to make man to be like Him. Because if fire has the power to change all things into itself and, having first destroyed in them all that is contrary to its nature, to transmute them into its own form and perfection, how much more will the consuming fire of God (Hebrews 12:29) destroy every impurity in our souls and transform them into His likeness?

> The more you are aware of God's love for you, the more you will be able to love God.

The God for whom the Christian entertains a fierce passion is not merely an external being far away. My passion for Him is a passion for what is divine in myself—for Christ who lives in me. This discovery of the divine jewel in yourself makes every day a Sunday for you. Most men are more generous on Sunday than on other days. This is the day on which they spend most on satisfying their own pleasure. Now you will spend your energy, your time, your liberty, your life, on God.

With this discovery, the old nature dies in you. It dies in

poverty. It never did possess anything worth mentioning. The dead are free from debt. Your mind is no longer burdened by the remembrance of past sins. They do not belong to you, but to another being who has passed away. You can speak of them as you would of a crime committed by some murderer three hundred years ago. It is not you. Your mind is free. Now you can judge before you act. And so you will see the salvation of the Lord.

We have from the Greeks the legend of Prometheus who stole fire from the gods and made possible the progress of humanity by giving the fire to men. Prometheus means "the one who thinks beforehand." Such a person is very rare. Most people are "Epi-metheus." They act under impulse, prompted by psychological complexes, fears, anxieties, and so on, which are all the result of past sin. Only afterward along comes the mind, liked a wicked stepmother, to tell you how wrong you have been.

But the discovery that Christ, the divine jewel, the hope of glory within your own heart, is Himself your real personality, sets you free from all this. For the first time you can begin to fulfill the commandment to serve God with all your mind. You are a true Prometheus. Your actions are well thought out beforehand. They are successful, as the Godhead is always successful. It succeeds even when it seems to be defeated, as it appeared to be on the cross. Such a life is worth living. You will sacrifice for it gladly and liberally, where once you did so grudgingly or not at all.

It is not extraordinary deeds, like going off as missionaries to arduous places, which make us Christians. It is our daily burnt offering and the abundance of our freewill offerings. To devote as a matter of course your thought, your time, your energy, your substance to the cause of God—which is your own cause because you are a partaker of the divine nature—this is true Christianity.

God, through Christ, united with a human body and made human life His own. So you now unite with Christ. His life is your real life, your ordinary everyday life. It was not an exceptional deed for Jesus to be human. He was human day by day, as a helpless babe, as a diligent schoolboy, as an obedient son, as a conscientious carpenter, as a faithful preacher and healer, as a martyr, in His weakness and despair as one who was separated from the Father. He daily shared all aspects of human life, including its temptations. He spent all his Godhead on human life. In the same way the child of God shares the whole of divine life. He does not express this life only in moments of emotional bliss and rapture. He carries out the ordinary things of life in a divine manner. In his routine occupations, in the home, in the workshop, in the scientific laboratory, in unavoidable failures of the flesh he spends himself as God would do, because God is a passion for which he gives up everything—because God has become his real being.

Prisons are full of men who suffer for passions such as gambling, stealing, or sexual vice. Why should we Christians not also suffer gladly for our passion? Amen.

CHAPTER 18

Prayer for the Dead

Dear brothers and sisters,

I have not preached to you for a long time. We have had a very bad time lately. Our jailers have behaved worse than ever. They filled our bellies with water and jumped on us. They hung some of us up by our thumbs. They tied us with crossed arms between two pillars and whipped us until we fell over fainting. Why did they tie our arms like this? It was with his arms in the same posture that Jacob blessed his grandchildren.

God is becoming, just as He wishes to be, less and less intelligible, a God who "would dwell in the thick darkness" (1 Kings 8:12, KJV). Let Him fulfill His desire. I leave Him in peace and do not disturb Him with my demands.

I have something better to do, to prepare myself for meeting Him. If things continue like this, I shall not last long. I shall die. They will bury my corpse.

The Trappist monks greet one another with the words, *"Memento mori*—remember you will die." As a spiritual exercise, I had formed the habit some time before my arrest of saying the burial service that we use in our church, imagining myself to be the one for whom it was spoken. At the end, I would sing Mozart's *Dies Irae*, composed in macabre circumstances. Legend says that, while writing it, he was visited by a mysterious stranger with the appearance of a skeleton. Catholics sing it at burials:

Day of wrath, O, day of mourning!
See fulfilled the prophets' warning!
Heav'n and earth to ashes turning!

O what fear man's bosom rendeth
When from heaven the Judge descendeth,
On whose sentence all dependeth...

When the Judge his seat attaineth
And each hidden deed arraigneth,
Nothing unavenged remaineth.

What shall I, frail man, be pleading,
Who for me be interceding,
When the just are mercy needing?...

Low I kneel, with heart submission,
See like ashes my contrition.
Help me in my last condition.

I have continued with this practice in my solitary cell though my mind often gets confused and it is difficult to remember the exact words.

There is something unique about a burial service. It is possible to imagine myself as a king (Napoleon started as a corporal and became an emperor), a bishop (St. Ambrose was chosen to be a bishop before he was even baptized), a millionaire (many poor people have become rich), or free. Such eventualities are all possible, and so we are able to imagine them. But to be dead is not possible for the human soul. Proof of this is the fact that we cannot imagine ourselves to be dead. I try to picture my death. I see myself lying still and cold in a coffin. But the fact that I see myself, and that I can even recite the burial service, shows that I am not very dead. A man should be serious during his spiritual exercises. Sometimes I roar with laughter. I am not dead, and never will be. "Whoever lives and believes in Me shall never die," said Jesus (John 11:26).

But I am no longer normal. I stop suddenly in the middle of my laughter and begin to cry, because the words of Jesus belong to some mysterious sphere of unintelligible truth. They don't correspond to reality. The fact is that Christians do die. Countless numbers of them have died under torture or otherwise over the centuries. And I may die very soon.

At this moment, people are praying for me. I am sure of this. Will they stop praying if, by chance, they hear that I have died? Will they stop praying for me just when I will need it the most?

In times past I have taken part in discussions on the subject of whether Christians should pray for the dead. People smiled as they debated. No one had in mind the moment of his own death. When death threatens you, you see things otherwise. Why should I be abandoned in prayers as soon as I die?

Because prayer for the dead is unscriptural? Many things that are unscriptural are still very good. You will not find family prayers mentioned in the Bible. Is this practice therefore wrong? The Bible mentions churches only in towns. Village churches appear to be unscriptural. Are they wrong? Is it scriptural to be Lutheran, or Baptist, or Catholic, or Orthodox?

Is it even certain that prayer for the dead is unscriptural? I remember a prayer in Nehemiah, which I often used in my devotions: "Do not let all the trouble seem small before You that has come upon us, our kings,...our fathers and on all Your people, from the days of the kings of Assyria until this day" (Nehemiah 9:32). The Jews had no kings in the time of Nehemiah. He mentions kings and Jewish ancestors long since dead.

In any case, I would think the same way even if there were verses which contradict this. The true interpretation of all Bible verses is love. "God is not the God of the dead, but of the living." He is the God of Abraham, Isaac, and Jacob (Matthew 22:32). In Hebrew, and even more clearly in Greek, it is said, "I am the God Abraham, the God Isaac and the God Jacob." He has identified Himself with these living dead. To abandon them means to abandon God Himself.

I don't know about others, but I, when I die, will need your prayers. I am saved, but even the children of God come to judgment. They will have to answer not only for every wrong deed, but even for an idle word. We will not go to hell for these sins, but God has punishments for His children also.

Mary was saved, but what a punishment it was for her, and for the other women who followed Jesus, to stand at the foot of the cross and to hear Jesus crying, "My God, My God, why have You forsaken Me?" (Matthew 27:46). Jesus at that moment did not know the answer to the question. Mary knew: He was forsaken for her sins. And she could not help Him. He had to pass through darkness and death because of her past sinfulness.

Peter was forgiven for his denials, but he had to bear a heavy punishment. He was asked three times by the Lord, "Do you love me?" (John 21:17). He was not trusted after his first answer —punishment enough for one who loved Him.

I have sinned so much, even since I became a Christian and a pastor. I need your prayers. I need the prayers of the glorified saints. Would it not influence the judgment at all if I could appear before the Lord surrounded by the prayers of thousands of children of God who would implore pity for my failures?

Whatever you think about prayers for the dead, pray for me. Pray what Nehemiah prayed for the Jewish kings and his forefathers who had died long ago, "Do not let all the trouble of Richard seem small before You. It is true that Richard has sinned much, but he has also had a very troubled life. He has suffered much. Oh, that his grief were fully weighed and his calamity laid with it in the balances. It would be heavier than the sand of the sea (Job 6:2,3). He has sinned, but he has received from Your hand double for all his sins (Isaiah 40:2). Let his sin be small before you, and his trouble great. For Jesus' sake, forgive him."

> I have sinned so much, even since I became a Christian and a pastor. I need your prayers.

God is sovereign. It depends on Him whether to see a thing as big or small. Paul decided to consider his terrible afflictions— the repeated jailings, beatings, stonings—as "light" (2 Corinthians 4:17). If we can consider our afflictions for God as light, could He not reciprocate by considering the sins of those who have suffered as light also? When I am overcome by worry, I begin to whistle quietly. Why should God ponder in detail about my sin? Simply by turning away His head He no longer sees it. So by a prayer of yours you could distract His attention from my sins; you might make Him turn His head toward you. My sins would not be observed anymore.

Live just once in the spirit your own burial service, even if you cannot recite it under such menacing conditions as ours. Then you will no longer philosophize about the question of prayers for the dead. You will think, "Poor man, he has died. Even now he may be passing through judgment. Let me make a desperate attempt to help him. I may not succeed. But neither can I harm him by my prayer."

Brothers and sisters, death is ready to swallow me. Pray for me. The German Lutheran Pastor Blumhardt asserts that he saw the souls of the dead in church imploring the prayer and fellowship of the living. I may not be normal anymore, but I have the same fancy. I see dead persons in my solitary cell, asking for my prayers. Luther objected only against public prayer for the dead, because of the abuses connected with it and the false hopes it might give, but not against private prayer for them. Pray for me.

Remember the words of Boaz, "that the name of the dead may not be cut off from among his brethren" (Ruth 4:10). Amen.

CHAPTER 19

Going Mad

BELOVED BROTHERS AND SISTERS,

The Bible speaks of "the foolishness of God" (1 Corinthians 1:25). The original Greek word has the meaning more of "stupidity"; our Romanian translators have used the word "madness." This madness of God's attracts me much more than His wisdom. And I will ask questions that may seem most impious: Has God always been mad like this, or did He become so by suffering too much pain? Is His madness curable? But these are mad questions, you will say. I agree. I cannot deceive myself; I am slowly going mad. So I cannot ask any questions other than mad ones. Well then, if I know this, why don't I keep quiet instead of asking questions? But He, too, knows about His madness, yet He still asks questions of us and gives us revelations.

I want to know all about His madness, because madness has become my lot.

A high percentage of mental patients are Jews. As pastor of a Hebrew Christian congregation, I had to deal with quite a number of cases. My wife nursed schizophrenics. I have read about this illness, so I know what is happening to my mind.

Schizophrenics withdraw from reality. Their only preoccupation is with inner fantasies. Well, all prisoners shut up in solitary cells develop these characteristics. We grow out of touch with the world. We live on our imagination, which is entirely different from that of men who lead a normal life. But what about God? He is *aghios*. This Greek word, which we translate as "holy," means literally "not of the earth" (*ghea*). It is a way of saying that God is out of touch with the realities of this earth. And as to His thoughts, He says Himself that they are not like ours (Isaiah 55:8). So, even by becoming mad, I become closer to His image. How trustfully a Christian can watch himself losing his mind!

My responses have become dulled. The guards shout. I sometimes, rarely, hear the screaming of prisoners who are being beaten. I continue to pursue my own line of thought. Gone is the time when I reacted by banging on the door or even weeping. God sees from heaven the tortures of His children. He hears their cries. He does not react either. What inconsistent behavior for a God as men imagine Him to be if they don't believe His own revelation about His foolishness.

My hands tremble all the time. I see no reason why they should. I suppose it is an image of God's hands, which tremble when He has to punish, because He loves the wicked man and cannot bear to see him destroyed.

Being constantly watched through the peephole, no wonder I have developed a persecution complex. I am afraid to touch the food. It might contain narcotics or poison. Jesus said unexpectedly to those "Jews who believed in Him" (John 8:31): "You seek to kill Me" (John 8:37). That looks like persecution mania. The curious thing is that those Jews, who believed in Him and whom He appeared to be falsely accusing of harboring murderous intentions, really did take up stones to cast at Him. So in the same heart there can co-exist belief in Jesus and the desire to kill Him. And the foolishness of God, which recognizes the latter desire in believers, is wiser than the wisdom of men. Perhaps my own persecution mania is also well-founded, and I do well to beware of men.

Being much persecuted, and my sick imagination making me exaggerate the extent to which I am in danger, produces a reaction in me. Why should I be persecuted, imprisoned, tortured, if I am not somebody important? Now I observe the delusions of grandeur growing in me. I hear voices strengthening me in such delusions. How sure Jesus was that He was the Messiah, though He knew that many others in the past had believed the same thing of themselves, but wrongly. If He was not the Messiah, why should Herod have tried to kill Him while He was still a babe in His mother's arms? Why all the anger against Him when He spoke and even when He healed? I, too, firmly believe in my delusions of grandeur. St. Augustine said, "We are Christ." What higher thing than this could I be? It is condescension on my part if I sometimes have fantasies of being merely some little earthly ruler or pope.

No, I do not have delusions of grandeur. I am grand. I can die today in this prison cell and suddenly have the wonders of God burst upon me. One of these wonders will be His kinship with me, even when I am mad.

The guards mock me. They call me "Hamlet in misery." Well, Hamlet was a prince, even though he was mad. Every day men share his tragedy and foolishness, and learn from it to be better. Who remembers the name of even one of Denmark's jailers of his time?

I don't mind going mad, and God does not mind having His foolishness proclaimed. No treatise of systematic theology mentions it among His attributes. It is contrary to reason to believe in a foolish God, but one plain text is worth a thousand reasons. And here is the text "the foolishness of God." In here I am becoming foolish, too.

A man must be mad to believe in a mad God. But here is the supreme test of faith.

A Canaanite woman appealed to Jesus to cure her sick daughter. He refused, saying that He was not sent but to the lost sheep of Israel. When she insisted, He called her a dog, saying, "It is not good to take the children's bread and throw it to the little dogs" (Matthew 15:26). I was revolted when I first read this. A healer who practices racial discrimination toward the sick is not worthy of the name of healer. Not only is He not divine, He is not even human. It is shameful to call somebody a dog because she belongs to another nation than yours.

It took me years to understand that Jesus was not using the word "dog" as an insult. It only seems so to us. The people of the East did not have the same attitude toward animals that we do. Among us, a man would mind very much if his father called him an ass. But Jacob praised his son Issachar by calling him "a strong donkey" (Genesis 49:14). Jesus was highly commending this woman. He saw with sorrow that the Israelites were lost sheep, whereas this woman was faithful, like a dog. He was ready to perform miracles for those who were lost. But a faithful dog, a soul as attached to Him as this Canaanite woman was, a person who had crossed racial barriers and appealed to Him, a Jew (even today Brahmins in India would prefer to see their son die than call in a doctor from among the pariahs), should not ask for wonders. She should bear quietly with the tragedies of life. Miracles are bread for children. It is not good to take it from them in order to give it to those who are already faithful, and should believe without seeing wonders. The word "dog" in Jesus' mouth is a compliment. But she continued to demand healing for her daughter, and the Lord agreed that some crosses are too heavy even for the faithful. He cured the sick child.

> I will quietly accept my growing madness. I may be a madman, but I am His.

To be like a dog—this is what being faithful means. A dog does not care about the character of its master. He may be a genius or an idiot, wise or foolish, a thief or a saint. He may treat the dog with affection or he may beat it—the dog will continue to watch the house, and fight with aggressors, and never cease to be a trustworthy companion.

Let the lost children of Israel find it objectionable to believe in a God who acknowledges His own foolishness. Dogs simply love God, whatever He is like, and whatever He does. This dog-like attitude is unreasonable in the eyes of men. They call Christians fools, and they are right. But we have become fools, and are going mad, in the knowledge that God has chosen the foolish things of the world (1 Corinthians 1:27). Though we are fools, progressing visibly toward madness, we do not despair. It is for us one more sure sign of our salvation.

God has suffered terribly because of the rebellion of His children. This drove Him to the mad solution of sacrificing His beloved Son for unworthy sinners. He did it out of love for us, but it is love to the point of folly. His madness will be cured when the wall of partition erected by sin has disappeared, and He is all in all; when His creation has entered once more into rest and His kingdom stretches from shore to shore.

Until then, I will quietly accept my growing madness. I may be a madman, but I am His. Amen.

CHAPTER 20

They Saw Jesus Only

DEAR BROTHERS AND SISTERS,

When the apostles "had lifted up their eyes, they saw no one but Jesus only" (Matthew 17:8).

You can look at things at many different levels. Suppose I look at myself in a good mirror. I see myself exactly as I am. But then I look in a magnifying mirror. Now I see my image distorted. I change the mirrors, using ones that magnify more and more, until I am looking through something that resembles huge lentils. I can no longer see my face, only the molecules of which it is composed. I am once again seeing myself without distortion, but at another level, the molecular one. I can continue with the operation until I see the molecules composed of atoms, and then the atoms composed of elementary particles. Or, conversely, I can look at a man standing in a crowd, while I am going up in an airplane. The crowd will become smaller and smaller, until in the end hundreds of men have converged into one point. They have become a single unity.

On the earthly level, there were six men on Mount Tabor: Jesus, Moses, Elijah, and the three disciples. You could see them as separate individuals. But if you are looking from above, from the level of spirituality, you see all individuals unified in Christ. So the apostles saw Jesus only—not the mighty prophets, not their companions, not themselves, but only Him in whom we all live.

The ovule from which Jesus was born had at first been simply organic matter. Then, at Mary's meeting with the archangel Gabriel, it became fertilized by the Holy Spirit with the heavenly seed. The holy One (Luke 1:35) came into existence. Jesus was once merely a thing. The embryo developed just like every other embryo, passing through the different phases of life, but He was the embodiment of the pre-existent Son of God. So in Him the human world and the Godhead could be seen united. He was both high priest and the sacrifice offered by the priest. He was the lamb of God and the lion of Judah. He was the Holy One and He was made sin. Angels ascended and descended upon him, but He was counted among the criminals. He was a carpenter and the King of kings. He was a man of sorrows, yet joyfully took part in marriage feasts and banquets of a very worldy sort, given and attended by publicans and sinners. He was a Jew with an open heart for Gentiles, rating the good Samaritan higher than a neglectful priest of His own race.

Ibsen's Peer Gynt, when he awoke from a lifetime of failure, realized that he had never been himself, except in the heart and dreams of Solveig, the girl who had loved him and waited for him all the years. We live in the sphere of illusion if we live the life of our little self. How can you isolate the self? Parts of plants and animals, of creatures other than yourself, continually renew your body. You think in a language formed by others long before you were born, and according to laws of logic established by Aristotle. Your mind is full of what you have learned from others in school, from newspapers and films, from conversations or from books. How much of your thoughts are really yours? You may have been born as an original, but now you are a copy, a representative of a social type; you think what your nation, your social class, your race, your gender, your religious denomination thinks. What individual thoughts or desires remain in you? Perhaps 0.00005 percent of what is you. You live the transitory life of a man of a certain social and psychological type in a certain age. Your true self waits for you in the thoughts and aspirations which your best friend Jesus experiences for you. He is the One in whom we also, torn apart by so many conflicting tendencies, become one.

A Christian sees only the One. In an apocryphal papyrus found at Oxyrrhinchus, Jesus is quoted as saying, "Cleave the stone and you will find Me within it. Cut the wood, and lo, I am within it." Nature receives its beauty from Him. He is mankind's ultimate aim. He is the King of the choirs of angels. He is the Beloved of the Father. In Him, God and creature become one.

It is said that the Japanese wanted to find a good market for their steel, which was of an inferior quality to the Swedish product. They named the town in which the steel industry was situated "Sweden," so that with a clear conscience they could then label all their products "Made in Sweden."

Our false self tends to do something similar. He will give himself a new name—he becomes a religious self, a spiritual self, a self faithful to Jesus, instead of denying himself totally and seeing "no one but Jesus only." Jesus in me, Jesus in my neighbor, Jesus in development in the torturer who beats me, Jesus in Moses and Elijah, Jesus in those yet to come, Jesus in nature, Jesus in all things.

During the war, my wife was away in another country on a very dangerous mission. There was no possibility of communication between us. All the time she was away, I could read nothing. On the pages of newspapers and books, I saw her image. I walked along the road and surprised myself by calling out her name. When the branch of a tree, shaken by the wind, knocked against my window during the night, I had the impression that she had returned and was knocking at the door. Her image persisted continually in the retina of my eye. This is what happens with Christians. They see in sinners and saints alike only what comes from Jesus. Like the Abbot Zosima in *The Brothers Karamazov*, they would bow before the criminal. He is made Christlike by the sorrows and sufferings which he prepares for himself through his wickedness. There is no place on earth where sparks of Christ are not spread around.

Shakespeare's Prospero says to Miranda that, by withdrawing from the world, he awakened his brother's evil nature. "My trust, like a good parent, did beget of him a falsehood in its contrary as great as my trust was." We criticize our bishops, priests, and pastors, without asking ourselves whether our shyness and trust might have created their untrustworthiness.

I have said that there is a way of looking up in which, although six people are present, you see no one but Jesus only. Why have you allowed your priests and pastors to give you less than this? Why have you accepted as a spiritual guide a man who does not see the One only, and is unable to direct your gaze in such a manner that you also see only One?

When you see in everybody only the One, the true Light that illuminates every man who comes into the world (John 1:9), you will no longer despise any man.

The Jewish scribes of old despised the common people. It is recorded in the Talmud that Rabbi Eleazar said, "It is lawful to kill a common man even on the Day of Atonement which falls on a Sabbath." Rabbi Samuel ben Nahmani said, "It is lawful to tear a common man to pieces like a fish." Jesus has taken such common men—fishermen, harlots, publicans—and has made them into saints and heroes by teaching them the great mystery of oneness. God is One. There is one Lord, one faith, one baptism. There is only One to be seen, to be looked upon. It was in looking not on the multitude of snakes crawling around them, but only on the one bronze serpent that the Israelites were healed (Numbers 21:9). As long as you see a multitude of men and things, you will always be afraid and troubled by their multitude; but Mary chose the good part, to sit at the feet of only One, the One in whom all the other twelve guests lived, the One who was the real Self of the twelve (Luke 10:42). She looked to Him only, lis-

> Jesus has taken such common men—fishermen, harlots, publicans—and has made them into saints and heroes.

tened to Him only. This part cannot be taken from you. In the multitude, every moment new things and new men are appearing and disappearing. But the One is eternal.

United with this One, you too are eternal. There will never be a time without this One. If He is your life, there will never be a time without you. We bear His name. So many people believe us to be Christians. Let us not put to shame those who have believed in us, but let us be what a Christian is meant to be: a Christ in miniature, a living part of the one great mystical body in which Jesus is the head and we are all members.

So long as I was still out in the world, surrounded by crowds of people, I was too weak to attain this state. He has given me the privilege of being put in a solitary cell. At least through this I have been able to learn what all Christians must learn, even when they are surrounded by multitudes of people—to "see no one but Jesus only." Amen.

Epilogue

THE CATHOLICS HAVE a hymn, "O, Felix Culpa—O, blessed guilt, which has given us a Savior." Some believe that I am anti-Communist in the vulgar political sense of the term. On the contrary, I am tempted to sing, "O, blessed Communists who have given us hours of voluptuous embraces with the heavenly Bridegroom, an insight into heavenly things that we never had before, victories of faith, not only under difficult outward circumstances, but through inner storms."

Countless thousands of people are in prison for Christ's sake in Communist countries today. It is not only the physical fact of being in prison, it is the shame. Joseph in the Old Testament, just because he wished to keep his purity, had to bear the humiliation of sitting in prison under the trumped up charge of adultery. Christians in the Red camp are accused of theft, treason, espionage, currency offenses and even of ritual murder. But, please, don't pity them. Don't pity the bride who has gone into the marriage feast leaning on the arm of her bridegroom. The Bridegroom loved the cross. She shares the joy of the cross with Him. Suffering is involved, but this is no reason to pity her.

When asked why I describe the atrocities of communism, I searched myself to discover my real motive for doing so. It is most of all to stir up your compassion for the Communists, who are burdening their poor souls with crimes.

I wish to stir up prayer for them, to call the churches to the task of spreading the life-giving gospel among the Communists. There is, of course, the other side. Christians must pray for and help the persecuted underground church. Well over one million letters of enthusiastic support, and the creation of missions to the persecuted church in over thirty countries, are proof that the rank-and-file Christians of all denominations are on our side.

We also have Christian leaders who support us, but these are fewer. Why the adverse attitude, or at least the apathy, of some?

It is, I think, first of all because they are theologians. Theology is a setting aside of *Theos*—of God Himself, who is not interested in doctrines but only wants our love—in order to dissect the *logos*, some hundreds of millions of words which have been written about the one Word of the living God: "Unite with me in love, forget about words in the reality of my embrace." *Theos*, God, makes you love. Theology has produced strife, hatred, and even murder.

Secondly, it is because these people carry the responsibility for vast church organizations, which can subsist as such only by adjusting themselves to successive political regimes. There was a time when Hitler's photograph was on the altars of some German evangelical churches, when certain Catholic and Protestant German pastors wore the uniform with the swastika, rather than face prison or death. In Communist countries, theologians have had to cheer Stalin and to praise the Soviet regime. There is a big difference between what an American Baptist pastor preaches in the South and what he says in the North when he touches on racial issues. I have heard a renowned pastor saying two different things according to the attitude of his audience, which in one state was in favor of segregation and in the other against it. Without this adjustment, the big religious organizations could not exist. Of this fact we must have full understanding.

But why do big religious organizations have to exist at all? St. Athanasius had the truth about the Holy Trinity. An ecumenical council disowned him and he was expelled from church membership under no less a trumped-up charge than of murdering a bishop and raping a virgin. He was told, "The whole world is against you," to which he replied, "Then I am against the whole world." It is only men of this caliber who have been canonized; only they are considered heroes of Christianity.

Happily, the underground church has no big structure to keep in existence. Even less do you have to worry about buildings, finances, and committees when you are alone in a solitary cell. There, only truth counts. You struggle to find it.

The story is told that a Japanese emperor once announced his intention of going to see a renowned garden of orchids. On the appointed day, his host met him at the gate and bowed respectfully. "Would His Imperial Majesty please to come into the garden first? Tea will be served afterward." They went into the garden, but the earth had been leveled. There was not a flower to be seen. The emperor did not say a word. Then he was invited into the house. On the tea table stood a vase containing one single orchid of unsurpassable beauty. The host said, "I have kept the most beautiful flower for the grandest of emperors. The other blooms did not deserve to live."

> Only the ultimate, eternal truth survives in the underground church.

Only the ultimate, eternal truth survives in the underground church. All other considerations that engage the transitory interests of a church disappear.

By joining hands with the underground church, Christianity in the free world will gain an influx of truth, love, and heroism. It is a question of life or death for Christians of countries that are not yet under the Communist yoke.

The purpose of this book, as of all my books, has been to familiarize children of God in the free world with what may be their own lot very soon—if communism and Islam continue to spread—and to bring them into the holy atmosphere of those who continue to believe when their faith is gone, who hope when they are in despair, who love even when they rebel, and who proclaim that God is King where Satan reigns. Will you too leave reason behind, and follow us into the realm of the foolishness of God which is shared by His suffering children—a foolishness which is wiser than men?

I wonder if you disagree with many of the thoughts expressed in this book. I, for my part, disagree. I told you what I thought then, not what I think now. I did it, because my "then" is the "now" of millions of men and women imprisoned for their faith in Communist countries today. You can share their sufferings only through knowing the torments of their minds.

I have done my part. I leave it to you. Choose to judge, to object, or to help.

I am happy also to render a service to my adversaries and to the opponents of my missionary work.

One of the men I respect most is a Catholic bishop with whom I was in prison. He once told me, "I wish to give you as a gift a very strong argument which you can use against my church. Christ has taught that when someone has sinned, he should say, 'Forgive us our trespasses,' when according to our doctrine he should have said to the offender, 'Go and confess to a priest.'" The bishop told me this, just because he loved Protestants.

Jump at this book, all my enemies and all the opponents of our mission. I make you a rich present. I give you here plenty of material to prove that I am a heretic, mad, and whatever else you like. Just profit by it. I love you. Why should you not have a little joy? You don't know the beauty of the embraces of the heavenly Bridegroom. Have at least the joy of attacking me.

But the children of God will understand. They will feel as if they themselves suffer today this terrible strain. The Bible teaches, "Remember the prisoners as if chained with them" (Hebrews 13:3). Manacles hurt not only the wrists, but also the soul. If this book will have caused some to shed a tear, to say a prayer, and to practically help the martyrs, my aim in publishing it will have been achieved.

Resources on The Persecuted Church

Other Books by Richard Wurmbrand
Tortured for Christ
Alone With God
100 Prison Meditations
The Oracles of God
In God's Underground
From Suffering to Triumph
Christ on the Jewish Road
In the Face of Surrender (formerly The Overcomers)
Victorious Faith
Reaching Toward the Heights
With God in Solitary Confinement
The Answer to the Atheist's Handbook
Marx & Satan

Other Books by The Voice of the Martyrs
The Pastor's Wife, *by Sabina Wurmbrand*
God's Missiles Over Cuba, *by Tom White*
The Spiritual Battle for Cuba, *by Tom White*
Between Two Tigers, *by Tom White*
A Window in Time, *by Tom White*

Videos by Richard Wurmbrand
Preserve the Word
No Other God
The Faces of God
To Shout or to Listen
Romania: The Return
In Prison With Psalm 107, *by Sabina Wurmbrand*

Videos by The Voice of the Martyrs

The Martyrs' Cry. James Jeda, a Sudanese boy; Ruth, a Vietnamese Hmong girl; Rikka, an Indonesian teenager. They live in different parts of the world, they've grown up in different cultures, but they share one thing in common. They are more than conquerors in some of the worst persecution known to man for their faith in Jesus Christ. "Join" your brothers and sisters in Sudan, Southeast Asia, and Indonesia as they testify to the sufferings they have endured and how their faith allowed them to hold fast to the Rock of Salvation. Filmed on location and hosted by CNN's David Goodnow, this video brings you face to face with your persecuted family. *The Martyrs' Cry* is adapted from the 1999 IDOP video *Four Faces* and includes additional footage. Don't miss this opportunity to "meet" your family!

Faith Under Fire. *Faith Under Fire* features interviews with Christians who face persecution head-on. You will meet a Muslim whose "road to Damascus" conversion leads to his persecution; a Chinese pastor suffering under the "strike-hard" policy that Christians now face; and a Vietnamese teenager dealing with her father's arrest and imprisonment for his work in the underground church. *Faith Under Fire* will challenge you to consider, "Is my faith ready to hold up under fire?" (Contains dramatic scenes that may not be suitable for children.)

Stephen's Test of Faith *(children's video)*. Twelve-year-old Stephen is mocked and ridiculed for his faith. That night in a dream, Stephen travels through history meeting Jesus, Stephen the martyr, families about to enter the Roman coliseum, William Tyndale, Christian children in today's Middle East, and others who dare to share their faith.

Filmed internationally, *Stephen's Test* is an inspiring challenge to all ages, a powerful tool for Sunday school, the unsaved, classrooms, your home. This walk with faithful heroes encourages us with their historical call to continue following Jesus Christ when we are put to "the test." (Includes study outline with Scripture references.)

The Voice of the Martyrs has available many other books, videos, brochures, and other products to help you learn more about the persecuted church. In the U.S., to request a resource catalog, order materials, or receive our free monthly newsletter, call (800) 747-0085 or write to:

> The Voice of the Martyrs
> P. O. Box 443
> Bartlesville, OK 74005-0443

If you are in Canada, England, Australia, New Zealand, or South Africa, contact:

> The Voice of the Martyrs
> P. O. Box 117
> Port Credit
> Mississauga, Ontario L5G 4L5
> Canada

> Release International
> P. O. Box 19
> Bromley BR2 9TZ
> United Kingdom

> The Voice of the Martyrs
> P. O. Box 598
> Penrith NSW 2751
> Australia

> The Voice of the Martyrs
> P. O. Box 69158
> Glendene, Auckland 1230
> New Zealand

> Christian Mission International
> P. O. Box 7157
> 1417 Primrose Hill
> South Africa

PASTOR RICHARD WURMBRAND is an evangelical minister who endured fourteen years of Communist imprisonment and torture in his homeland of Romania. Few names are better known in Romania, where he is one of the most widely recognized Christian leaders, authors, and educators.

In 1945, when the Communists seized Romania and attempted to control the churches for their purposes, Richard Wurmbrand immediately began an effective, vigorous "underground" ministry to his enslaved people as well as the invading Russian soldiers. He was arrested in 1948, along with his wife, Sabina. His wife was a slave-laborer for three years on the Danube Canal. Richard Wurmbrand spent three years in solitary confinement, seeing no one but his Communist torturers. He was then transferred to a group cell, where the torture continued for five more years.

Due to his international stature as a Christian leader, diplomats of foreign embassies asked the Communist government about his safety and were informed that he had fled Romania. Secret police, posing as released fellow-prisoners, told his wife of attending his burial in the prison cemetery. His family in Romania and his friends abroad were told to forget him because he was dead.

After eight-and-a-half years in prison, he was released and immediately resumed his work with the Underground Church. A couple of years later, in 1959, he was re-arrested and sentenced to twenty-five years in prison.

Mr. Wurmbrand was released in a general amnesty in 1964, and again continued his underground ministry. Realizing the great danger of a third imprisonment, Christians in Norway negotiated with the Communist authorities for his release from Romania. The Communist government had begun "selling" their political prisoners. The "going price" for a prisoner was $1,900; their price for Wurmbrand was $10,000.

In May 1966, he testified before the U.S. Senate's Internal Security Subcommittee and stripped to the waist to show the scars of eighteen deep torture wounds covering his torso. His story was carried across the world in newspapers throughout the U.S., Europe, and Asia. Wurmbrand was warned in September 1966 that the Communist regime of Romania planned to assassinate him; yet he was not silent in the face of this death threat.

Founder of the Christian mission, The Voice of the Martyrs, he and his wife traveled throughout the world establishing a network of over thirty offices that provide relief to the families of imprisoned Christians in Islamic nations, Communist Vietnam, China, and other countries where Christians are persecuted for their faith. His message has been, "Hate the evil systems, but love your persecutors. Love their souls, and try to win them for Christ."

Pastor Wurmbrand is the author of several books, translated into over sixty languages throughout the world. He has been called the "Voice of the Underground Church." Christian leaders have called him a living martyr and "the Iron Curtain Paul."